■ WHERE

THE

RIVERS

RAN

BACKWARD

■ WHERE

THE

RIVERS

RAN

BACKWARD

WILLIAM E. MERRITT

THE UNIVERSITY OF GEORGIA PRESS

ATHENS AND LONDON

© 1989 by William E. Merritt

Published by the University of
Georgia Press
Athens, Georgia 30602

Copyright credits for lyrics
reprinted in this book appear
on page 291.

All rights reserved

Designed by Richard Hendel

Set in Century Old Style

The paper in this book meets the
guidelines for permanence and
durability of the Committee on
Production Guidelines for Book
Longevity of the Council on Library
Resources.

Printed in the United States of America

93 92 91 90 89 5 4 3 2 1

Library of Congress Cataloging in
Publication Data

Merritt, William E.
Where the rivers ran backward /
William E. Merritt.
    p. cm.
ISBN 0-8203-1107-3 (alk. paper)
1. Merritt, William E. 2. Vietnamese
Conflict, 1961–1975—Personal
narratives, American. 3. Soldiers—
United States—Biography. 4. United
States. Army—Biography. I. Title.
DS559.5.M46 1989
959.704'38—dc 19
[B]
88-22043
CIP
British Library Cataloging in Publication
Data available

To Elizabeth,

who taught me how to

love children.

In the hope that

you won't read this until

you are much older.

■ CONTENTS

■ PROLOGUE

■ INDUCTION STATION

Mrs. Brentnall is making me write this, and it is the truth. She told me to get it down—what I could remember. What it was like.

Well, I can remember quite a bit, thank you.

I joined the army in a rush to beat the draft. I went in on St. Valentine's Day 1968. Early that morning I drove down to the Armed Forces Entrance and Examination Station on Caine Street. The doors were jammed with peace demonstrators. Draft dodgers out to stop a war that might grab at them, out to stop the war by bullying me. They crouched on the steps and tore at my clothes like blackberries when I tried to get through. A gray struggle in the morning twilight.

Inside was bleak as a jail. No one to meet me. Just a sign.

INDUCTEES, FOLLOW RED LINE TO
PROCESSING AREA.

The ceiling was gray. The floor was brown. The walls were dirty green. No color except the five dull lines of chipped paint that followed each other down the hall like colored wires in a phone cable. Everything smelled of wax.

I followed the lines into the big building, my footsteps echoing down the corridors. It was a hike. Eventually one line turned off. I wondered who would turn with it.

DRAFT DODGERS, FOLLOW YELLOW STRIPE TO EXIT.

At the end of the corridor: steps. Four lines on each. Around the landing and up to another floor, where the path doubled back the way it had come, deeper into an alien place. Then another line turned away.

DRAFT AVOIDERS (TEACHERS, MARRIEDS),
FOLLOW THE DULL GRAY LINE

Then another.

CANDIDATES FOR HARDSHIP, PSYCHIATRIC, OR SECTION 13,
DISCHARGES FOLLOW DIRTY PINK LINE

Then my line veered left and passed under a door, where it
ended. A counter at the front of the room facing rows of dirty
school desks. Initials and names and hateful comments inked into
raw wood. Broken fluorescent lights flickering overhead. Nothing
to do for hours and drabness to break a heart.

An empty day spent in a hard seat, filling out forms. Of all the
pieces of paper, only one made much difference, the one for choos-
ing a combat arm. And that one made a great deal of difference
indeed.

I went down the blank list. Caught dead center at a genuine
fulcrum point in my life, I did not know enough to decide. A choice
to save my life, and all I had to draw on were impressions. Biases.
It was like ordering from a French menu, trying to guess what
would come from the sound of the names.

ARMOR. Lunging through green countryside. Noisy, creeping
targets surrounded by invisible enemies.

ARTILLERY. Crouching in lightly defended fire bases. Attracting
notice with every shot.

INFANTRY. Hip deep in rice and nowhere to hide.

SIGNAL. Standing on ridge lines. Bold silhouettes with flags—
until a black-clad sharpshooter interrupted communications.

That left the Corps of Engineers. I knew what they did. I had
seen their benchmarks in the Smokies and heard about the dams
out West. Whatever they did in Vietnam had to be better than what
the other combat arms did.

So I went to war as an Engineer. Close enough to watch but far
enough away to put it all behind me at night.

At the end of the day, I followed the red line back to the door.
Outside it was dark. The demonstrators had moved on.

■ LAMBERT FIELD

Not long afterward I waited at Lambert Field.
The army had handed me a ticket to Fort Leonard Wood, Missouri. Eastern to St. Louis, then off the jet and a long wait at the Ozark gate.

Not much entertainment in waiting, so I wandered off to see the airport. A boring place, as it turned out. Not a patch on Atlanta. But it did have one thing no other airport had. It had the original *Spirit of St. Louis* hanging up near the ceiling. From the balcony, you could look the plane in the eye. You could see the tread on the tires and the odd foreign decals pasted on the fuselage.

And the blind cockpit. There is no glass in the front of that plane. No windshield. The entire cockpit is as opaque as the tail assembly. Lindbergh couldn't see out. He flew blind all the way to France, an eyeless symbol of American technological achievement.

And that airplane is not alone. It hangs close enough to shoot down with a spitball, a national treasure comparable to the first Mercury space capsule or the original Edison phonograph, a treasure too important to stay in only one place at one time—and so we have another. Nestled alongside the Wright flyer (which looks exactly like the one on display down at Kitty Hawk), the *Spirit of St. Louis* also hangs at the Smithsonian.

The plane at Lambert Field—the plane that inspired me and probably a few score thousand other young soldiers, with the bright history of our own cultural daring—must be false coin.

But the inspiration still seems right.

■ RECEPTION STATION

An army bus carried me to the reception station. A counter, a vinyl-covered sofa, and a bored corporal who checked me in, issued me sheets, a blanket, and a mattress, and aimed me at a distant building. It was a long, biting walk in the cold Missouri winter, dribbling mattress all the way.

The building was all one big room filled with people I wasn't comfortable with. Hard southern whites, like some I knew back home, tough southern blacks, like some I'd met, and there were northerners: whites with hideous, aggressive accents who probably stole things. And mean blacks with big knives. I couldn't yet see that they were all as out of place as I was.

During the dark of the next morning, a sergeant taught us how to tie our shoes and how to brush our teeth and how to make our beds. An odd occupation for a grown man, if you ask me.

Later we stood shivering outside the supply room, our fatigues still creased from their packages and our long civilian hair curling over our green collars. The sergeant organized us into an icy knot and herded us off to an old-fashioned barber shop in a one-story frame barrack painted white.

Four at a time, we went in. Four at a time we came out to stand miserable, our shaved heads naked to the winter. Inside were four kindly-looking civilian barbers, all prepared to talk about yesterday's game in the ancient tradition of barbers. And they asked you—they actually asked you—"How do you want it?"

And we said, "A little off the top, please. Trim around the ears. Not too short in back."

Then they ran their razors over our heads with a deftness born of years of disregard while our locks fell to join others on the floor. We left a pile big enough to stuff a sofa.

We paid as we left. Full civilian rates, too, just as if the barbers had used care and artistry. Back outside we joined the rows of other shaved heads standing like cantaloupes in a furrowed garden.

The next day, they counted our teeth. A corpsman took inventory. The results went on a neat chart, and that was the extent of our dental care in the army. At discharge, two years later, we got a free trip to a civilian dentist. Anything in our mouths that wasn't on our charts was officially "service connected" and was fixed by the government.

That arrangement made the war cheaper. The VA picked up the tab, and the dental work didn't come out of the military budget. And there was less work to do that way, too. Things being what they were, a lot of mouths never returned home to apply for treatment. And the charts had another purpose. A use to suit the army. Careful dental records reduced the number of unidentified bodies in the Vietnam War to the point where it became almost impossible to find an unknown soldier.

■ MARCHING

I had hiked a lot as a kid, and I had the typical hiker's stride: bounce . . . step, bounce . . . step. It seemed a natural enough way to walk, but the army had different thoughts on the matter. We were to crunch along, head level, legs swinging in time like the blades of a paper shredder at the Pentagon. Most of the men picked it right up. They all stepped out together, their knees all bent together, and their heels made little crescents in the dust, all at the same time.

> Trip
> Trap
> . . . .
> Trip
> Trap

After we had passed, a dirt road looked like an unrolled bolt of some brown polka-dotted fabric. Row after row after neat row of brown marks retreating into a precise machine-made infinity.

All except for a slight wavy pattern just off the center. Little crescents that had missed their rows. My marks.

We marched to music. The solo voice of a sergeant, tenor or bass that could carry on for hours, turning numbers into musical cadences to strike the ground by.

> TOOP . . .
> THREEP . . .
> FOURP . . .
> YO LEP . . .
> TO LEP . . .
> YO LEP RIGHT LEP . . .

But my heels always struck the ground forward of the line that all the other heels had agreed upon, and the sergeants began to notice me. They accused me of diddly bopping. I didn't want to stand out, but I couldn't seem to settle my pace and just walk level, with my heels clicking in line.

YO[bounce]LEP . . .
YO[bounce]LEP . . .
YO[bounce]LEP [bounce]RIGHT[bounce]LEP . . .

When I tried, my rhythm accelerated, and there would be colli-
sions and stumblings in the ranks.

Sergeants treat diddly bopping as a moral flaw that can be cured
by criticism. They were experienced in criticism, and they tried
hard. But they really didn't have a chance.

When the sergeants realized they couldn't cure my diddly bop-
ping, they removed it. A classic flanking maneuver. They exiled me
to follow along behind the formation with the medical kit. To walk—
not march, but walk—with bandages and iodine in case anybody fell
out wounded. Nobody ever did, but it was fun back there, watching
everybody stepping so fine and listening to their cheerful singing in
counterpoint with the sergeants who, glad that their formation was
now regular, had forgotten the soldier with the medical kit diddly
bopping along behind.

"If I die on the PT test . . ."
"IF I DIE ON THE PT TEST."
"Bury me at the leaning rest . . ."
"BURY ME AT THE LEANING REST."

■ CAMOUFLAGE

One afternoon, after marching all morning through the pretty Ozarks—through the dust and over the ice and rocks—the sergeants pointed us down a hill.

"Stay on the trail, but look all you want."

We could see shaded bleachers nestled among the trees a couple of hundred meters down the path.

"There are six menses out there, in full combat gear. So close you could stand on the trail and hit every one of them with a cigarette butt. They's Charlies waiting to ambush you. Find their asses on the way down."

A piece of cake. A snap. Except only there wasn't anybody there. Nobody. Within a hundred meters of the trail was nothing but open land populated by odd clumps of brush, too scraggly to hide a cat. I searched back to the tree line.

"Not there, you dufous mother. They're not way the hell over in the trees. There. Next to the trail.

"LOOK NEXT TO THE MOTHER FUCKING TRAIL."

But they weren't next to the trail. At least not the trail we were on.

We gave it up and sat in the bleachers and waited for the sergeants to let us in on the joke. They did.

"Mr. Charlie done had himself a field day. Every one of you gentlemen's just been KIA'd.

"OKAY, OUT THERE. YOU MENSES CAN GET UP NOW."

Six men with helmets, packs, and rifles, dressed in fatigues and pieces of brush, materialized not more than a meter or two from the trail. They might as well have beamed down from a starship.

They stood in front of us, four white soldiers with green and black grease on their faces and two black soldiers in eerie silver and green paint.

It scared the holy shit out of me. There was a real war going on, and I was going to be in it. I kept remembering a movie I had seen as a kid in which the captain of a cruiser ordered the entire crew:

"Get down on your knees. All hands get down on your knees and thank almighty God those targets you couldn't hit today were not Japanese destroyers."

10

Ordinarily they drove us back in trucks from our outings in the woods, but that night we marched.

"If I die in a combat zone . . ."
"IF I DIE IN A COMBAT ZONE,"
"Box me up and send me home. . . ."
"BOX ME UP AND SEND ME HOME."

All the way back I kept thinking the Viet Cong probably knew camouflage better than those people did.

Get down on your knees.

Get down on your knees, and thank almighty God those soldiers at the side of the trail were Americans.

■ TALKING BACK

R aise your hand before you speak."
   "Talk quietly."
   "Don't answer until I call on you."
   The army liberated me from sixteen years of schoolteachers. Of being bossed by stuffy women. It was a liberation too long in coming. Now it was run and yell and shoot and curse. Kind of a regimented recess all day long. Teachers didn't like guns and knives, and they punished you for raising your voice. The army gave you a rifle and a bayonet and lots of yelling. The sergeants thought it was a sign of spirit. They would shove their noses next to yours and order you to do something preposterous. And you could answer back. You could yell in their faces. As long as the words came out "YES, SERGEANT," you could say anything you wanted. And what you said, and what everybody mostly said, was "FUCK YOU, SERGEANT." Right in their faces. As loud as we could.

If you yelled it loud enough, you had spirit and you were applauded. The army differs from school there. The army recognizes spirit.

Sometimes you could even get the words tangled up with the thought. And survive. Once a ratty soldier a couple of paces to my left actually yelled "FUCK YOU, SERGEANT."

Those words hung on the cold Missouri air as clear as the doomed soldier's breath while the sergeant wheeled around like a tracked vehicle turning toward a target. We all stood quiet, waiting for the explosion.

"WHAT DID YOU SAY TO ME, DICK HEAD?"

The soldier stood his ground.

"YOU HEARD ME, SERGEANT. I DIDN'T STAMMER. I SAID: 'YES, SERGEANT.'"

Quiet fell while we waited.

And waited.

And waited.

But nothing happened. The sergeant just walked on. He must have thought it was funny, too.

To this day, as I stand at parade rest in front of long desks giving reports to dull-eyed bosses, I see ranks of young men waiting in the Missouri cold and wish I could scream out my words an inch or two from the faces on the other side of those desks.

■ FOOD

Winter mornings were dark and frozen. Sometimes we stood in line for two hours before they let us into the mess hall. Inside it was warm and humid, and our cold glasses fogged over.

Serving lines and a riot of food. Thousands of fried eggs gliding in some unknown oil, staring up at us like creatures in tidal pools. Striped ribbons of bacon heaped in brick-colored strata, reams of toast, gravelly lakes of grits, all arranged in layers on our steel trays by apprentice cooks.

It was an extravagance. You would never see such food in your home. Not if you added up all the years of your life. That food came as good and as abundant as a bountiful nation could provide. Every day, privates unloaded wheels of cheese the size of truck tires. And mountains of spotless potatoes. And bacon. And fruit. And sacks of flour bigger and clumsier than reception station mattresses. And cans of vegetables we couldn't get our arms around. Cans a squad of Viet Cong could have eaten out of for a week. And eggs stacked by the thousands like crates of Ping-Pong balls in factory warehouses. And cut branches with single bunches of grapes it took two men to carry.

And they didn't just come to our mess hall. They flowed into every mess hall at every American outpost every day in a rolling Mississippi of food and treasure unmatched throughout the world and across time.

■ GI PARTY

We trained all day, and we cleaned all night. Sometimes we cleaned our brass, and sometimes we cleaned our boots, but mostly we cleaned the barracks. We'd take big brushes and soap the concrete floor and metal walls and scrub all the dirt and all the potential dirt and all the places where dirt might muster in the future. The place was clean when we started. And when we were done and it had dried, it didn't look any different.

The sergeants never explained why they had us spend so much time kneeling in soapy water. But later, one told me they wanted to see us enthusiastic and working together. They figured that if we bonded together in Basic, we wouldn't desert each other under fire. They imagined we were learning courage, swinging those big brushes.

We wouldn't have cared about that. We weren't going to be assigned to the field with each other anyway. We were all headed to war alone. The first war America ever fought that way, and if God loves us, it will be the last.

We would clean all week, and we would clean again Friday night. Then, on Saturday morning, a starched young lieutenant would stroll through, finding dirt.

His first few inspections were dry runs. Practices for us to get the hang of cleaning and, I've always believed, for him to get the knack of inspection. We trained each other, but we cleaned for our own reasons. We were scrubbing our way out of Basic. We cleaned because, if we cleaned enough, one bright Saturday morning we would have a real inspection and, if we passed, we could all go into Waynesville or St. Louis or any damn where else we pleased. As long as we passed that inspection.

That was our dream: to get out of the army for a weekend. To see our wives. To see our girlfriends. To spend the night in a motel in Waynesville. The reservations were all made. The deposits were paid. The tickets were bought. Until that Saturday we cleaned and polished and scrubbed. Then for a few precious hours we would be alone. Private parties with no sergeants and no other guys. Just bury our faces in sweet, beloved womanflesh until Sunday night.

15

FREE AT LAST!
FREE AT LAST!
Thank God a'mighty,
I'M FREE AT LAST!

■ HAND TO HAND

Y OU MUST BECOME YOUR ENEMY."
The sergeant was black, but he fancied himself Japanese.
"You must get inside of him. It's not enough to study him
and understand him. When it's just you and Charlie alone, staring
into each other's faces, the one that comes home is the one that
crawls into the other's skin like his own uniform. You have to look at
yourself through his eyes. Feel his hesitations. You must become
your enemy and
"YOU MUST KILL HIM.
"DO YOU UNDERSTAND?"
"Yes, sergeant."
"GOD DAMN IT. I ASKED YOU A QUESTION. DO YOU UNDER-
STAND?"
"YES, SERGEANT."
"That's better.
"Your body is the only weapon Charlie can't take away from you.
I'm going to teach you how to use it. It's your blade. Stick it in his
ribs. It's your club. Smash his nuts when his back's turned. Ain't
nobody fighting fair in this war."
We were standing in pairs in what looked like sawdust-filled horse-
shoe pits, each of us Charlie to the other. We circled for openings,
trying out the new tricks we'd learned. It wasn't real hand-to-hand
fighting, just isolated moves from karate and judo and Brooklyn.
Whatever somebody thought would work.
"If you've got anything on you—a pencil, a set of keys—stab
him in the eye."
"ONE EYE, SERGEANT?"
"The other will get all teary. You'll have thirty seconds to diddy-
mao the area before he can see again. You'll be long gone by that
time, Troop."
"If you've got a newspaper, roll it up and jab him beneath the
ribs. He'll be sucking dust after you've gone."
"A NEWSPAPER? In I Corps?"
"*STARS AND STRIPES*, TROOP. YOU'LL BE SEEING A LOT OF IT
WHERE YOU'RE GOING."
People study karate for years and feel like they don't know it well　17

enough to use it. We practiced hand to hand for a morning, and I felt like it would be worth a try if I were ever jumped by a lone VC, both of us unarmed and me with a copy of the *Stars and Stripes* in my hand. Maybe I'd be coming back from the latrine.

I would have gotten an afternoon of hand-to-hand training, too, but I had a doctor's appointment that day. The sergeants marked my record to show I'd gotten the training anyway. They calculated that was just as good.

It didn't make any difference. They weren't really teaching us hand-to-hand combat. They were selling us charms to ward off fear.

"Man for man, you're bigger and stronger and tougher than Charlie."

For a morning, we believed. And we'd never get the chance to find out different. Charlie didn't take prisoners. At least not enlisted prisoners. All those people's soldiers just shot enlisted men. The only prisoners they took were officers.

But still, the training did build confidence. And for a little while we believed we were as tough as the enemy. The charm didn't last, but for a time it pushed back the fear.

■ GUARD DUTY

The week before our first pass, the new guard duty roster was posted. I was down for Thursday night. Real guard duty. Outside with live rounds. I felt like a soldier.

Thursday came. We trained late, learning about concertina wire. Then we went straight to supper. Afterward I was fitted out for guard detail. Rifle. Helmet. Boots. And ammo. Five hard brass cylinders dropped into my hand.

Five blanks.

"Bring these back or fill out a report on each one."

Then wait outside in the dark.

A truck rolled out of the cold.

"Hop in, white bro. You gonna be gettin some OJT for Vee Et Nam.

"Slide your piece back of the seat, if you please. Something like that go off up here blind me, and this here deuce-and-a-half come to a stop in that ditch on the wrong side of the road over there. Took my bro's stripe for that once.

"Shee-it, bro, it's cold out there. Don't go taking no leaks tonight. Your piss'll freeze so fast you'll have a piece of ice jammed up your dick like a coat hanger wire. Save yourself for Nam, it's warm over there. You'll like it."

He let me off in the woods. A very important installation to be set off so in the wilderness. Like Los Alamos or a DEW line station.

I could just see the trail I was to follow. It wound around the side of a hill, twelve minutes a circuit. I could not tell what was at the center.

Round and round.

Nobody was watching me. Just my sense of duty to keep me walking that trail.

My sense of duty lasted about half an hour. Then I went exploring.

I scuffled down the hill to find this thing I was guarding. And stumbled into it before I saw it: an old clump of machinery glinting dully in the starlight. I ran my gloves over it, trying to decipher its purpose. And then I knew.

It was the gutted carcass of an overturned jeep. And off to the   19 side was the rusted frame of some broken piece of construction equipment. And that was it. Two rotting pieces of iron left there, no doubt, sometime before I was born. Scrap not worth dragging out of the woods. Wreckage that couldn't have been hauled off without a crane. And it wouldn't have taken me to spot a crane moving into the area. And five blanks wouldn't have stopped it.

I climbed back up the hill and sat on a rock, kicking my feet to keep warm. I wondered if any other nation on earth prepared its men for jungle warfare this way.

A cold hour and a half later, I heard Landis Green coming up to me in the dark. I recognized his voice. He had the bunk next to mine and we talked a lot. I told him about growing up in Atlanta. He told me about missing growing up in Chicago. I thought he was my buddy.

"Get your white ass in the truck, mofo. They's two of us out here and they's only one of you, and I don't know for sure if that other brother's carrying blanks."

"Green, is that me you're talking to?"

"Move, honky. I'm relieving you out here. Get in the mofo truck."

"What the hell you coming on like that for, anyway?"

"You jiving, mofo? Shee-it. Everybody in the barracks know. Everybody in the world know. How come you the only one don't know?"

"I haven't been in the barracks since seven o'clock this morning. They sent me here straight out after supper."

"Shee-it, mofo. You mofo lucky they sent me along. Some white dude. SOME WHITE MOTHER FUCKER DONE SHOT KING. Blowed him off a balcony in a cheap-ass hotel in Memphis. Shee-it."

Honk . . . HONNKKKK

"I tell you something, mofo. The evil dudes don't be shooting no blanks. They always gots the real thing. Now get in the truck."

"My God. I used to see him around Atlanta. Bump into him places. Saw him over Christmas in the lobby of the Paramount. He . . . "

HONNNNNNNNKKKKKKKKKKKKKK

"Go on. Get in the truck. I told that brother not to be messing with you."

It wasn't until I saw Green the next morning that I knew we were still friends. He just hadn't wanted any white dude to see him in his darkness.

■ FIRST PASS

The bright Saturday morning finally came. Our buttons were polished, our shoes were shined, our toilet articles marched across our lockers, and our bunks were as square as if they'd been surveyed. A lieutenant, looking dainty in white gloves, stepped through the barracks, delicately touching the intimate undersides of our gear. He found nothing. Nothing. We were as perfect as the guards at the Tomb of the Unknown Soldier.

While a hundred fires burned the cities of America, we had spent our Friday night in small things. Cleaning and arranging. We were the only barracks on post that morning without a single demerit. We may have been the only barracks that way in the whole free world.

We never again had so many sweet wives and sweethearts waiting outside to inspire us.

The lieutenant congratulated us and we were free.

> FREE AT LAST!
> FREE AT LAST!
> Thank God a'mighty,
> I'M FREE AT LAST!

The radio had played the same spiritual all weekend.

When the sergeant came in, we crowded around for our passes.

"You ain't going nowhere."

"WHAT?"

"I said: they ain't going to be no passes."

"Come on, Sarge. You heard what the lieutenant said. We did fine. Nobody else ever got a perfect score."

"You ain't neither. You just pass. That lieutenant, he new. He don't know what to look for. Koepke, you got dust on your bedsprings. He never even saw. Shee-it. So much shit on that window, it be like axle grease. He'd a have to throw them fancy gloves away if he touch it."

"I don't give a good God damn about your GOD DAMN dirt, Sarge. I ain't seen my old lady in seven weeks. You can hang my

21

ass for desertion come Monday, but I'm leaving here with or without your GOD DAMN pass."

"SIT DOWN, ROBBINS.

"The rest of you menses, listen up.

"Those dudes outside ain't playing. Leave this place in your greens, and you going to be cut up so bad your old lady ain't going to recognize none of the parts. They be burning the country down out there. White dude offs King on Thursday, black dudes off everybody else on Friday. And they be killing your green ass on Saturday if you carry it out to them. Ain't nobody here except for me got civilian clothes, and I ain't going nowhere. I don't got no wigs. Those mother fuckers see my regulation haircut, it don't make no difference I'm a brother. Maybe make things worse. They go calling me Oreo and cutting my black ass to see how white I am inside.

"You get your pass next week. Or the week after. You just pray you've still got a crèche to go back to."

"They ain't going to be no next week, man. How'm I gonna pay for my old lady to come all the way back down here from Motown again? You tell me that."

"You ain't gonna be paying nothing you be dead, Troop.

"You going to get passes lets you into the club. Only friend you gots right here. You be as safe patrolling alone through the Iron Triangle as you be outside. Do your drinking over to the club. You won't be catching no diseases there, neither."

"So how our old ladies going to find us there?"

"Cans't. They gots the perimeter sealed just like we be camping in the Ashaus."

"GOD DAMN IT, SERGEANT. GOD DAMN IT AND YOUR ROTTEN ASS BLACK HIDE. FUCK THAT MOTHER FUCKING CLUB SHIT. YOU CAN FIND ME AND MY OLD LADY IN WAYNESVILLE IF YOU'VE GOT THE BALLS TO COME LOOKING FOR US."

"You be wearing you dog tags then, Sampson. Just so's we can identify the body."

In the end, Sampson and Robbins and Koepke and the rest of us spent the weekend crowded into the club, swallowing warm beer and talking about the ladies trapped outside. And listening to the radio.

FREE AT LAST!
FREE AT LAST!
Thank God a'mighty,
I'M FREE AT LAST!

■ QUICK KILL

The civilian stood in front of us, plocking coins out of the air with a BB gun. The toss, and the coin would arc smoothly into the air. One shot from the hip and it would tumble into the dust.

He commented as he shot.

"Shoot from the hip. That's all the time you gonna get. You're lucky when you get that.

"You think the Cong's gonna stand up there for you all nice and steady like a target on the rifle range so you can sight in on him from between your sandbags? Never happen. All you're gonna see of the Cong is the muzzle flash from his AK47 when he unloads on you up some jungle trail. If you don't fire from the hip, you won't be firing at all, I can tell you that."

When he stopped to pick up the coins, the usual sergeant took over.

"You heard the man. Today, you be learning to shoot from the hip. By this afternoon every one of you be picking nickels out of the air. Some of you be hitting dimes. If you can hit a nickel, you can hit a Charlie. Nickel ain't nowhere near to as big."

Then the civilian spoke back up.

"Gentlemen, I've been training bird hunters most of my life, and I'll tell you something. Hunting a quail is no different from hunting a Cong. You and a few buddies are walking through an empty field. You're looking and you're listening, but you can't see a thing. Then they're in your face. You do the same thing in Nam you do in an old brushy patch here in Missouri. You point at the nearest one and you shoot. Then you point at the next one and you shoot again.

"You notice I said 'point,' not 'aim.' You don't have any time to fart around with aiming. You point at your target and pull the trigger. Forget about squeezing. Just pull it.

"Pick a tree or a rock or something off in the distance, and point your finger at it. Now sight down that finger. What do you see? Unless you move your finger, you see what you pointed at. Your finger is a dead shot. All you have to do is point that finger at the Cong and fire. Bang. He's a dead Cong.

"That's what we do out here with these little BB guns—just line   23 our fingers up along the barrel and point at the coin. Bang. Dead coin. Every time.

"Okay, everybody, come down here and take one of those BB guns."

"HONYO FEET."

"Thank you, Sarge."

"We'll start with quarters. Now pair up. One of you toss, the other point and shoot. From the hip, like big John Wayne."

"Toss it out in front of yourself, dufous, so's you don't get shot, too."

"Another trick. The BB drops. So will your bullet. Point at the top of your target."

The quarters fell like sprayed flies. When nickels and finally pennies tumbled from the air, we were all trick shots. But it was only another charm to ward off fear. Viet Cong weren't quail. You didn't flush them. They opened up on you from behind trees and rocks and stumps. When that happened, you weren't thinking about standing in the middle of a trail, rifle to hip, pointing back at them. You were on your stomach, thinking about cover. When you reached it, you used your angry black weapon as you had been taught on the rifle range.

It was strange, hiring civilians to teach soldiers to use army weapons. As if the army had lost confidence in itself. But it was a strange war. A war in which the military gave over all its thinking to civilians. And civilian decisions were mostly moral judgments. Civilians decided what weapons could be used. They dictated targets that could be bombed, and they directed where the army could send troops. And each civilian decision was the result of a painstaking analysis of every conceivable moral duty.

Every moral duty, that is, except the duty to support our people in the field.

■ AIT

B asic ground to a sullen ice-choked conclusion and then we processed through to AIT: Advanced Individual Training, the time when the army would make us into Engineers. When it would teach us to build. To change the course of streams and to leave our marks on mountains.

AIT turned out to be like Basic, only the weather was warmer.

■ LAYING TRACK

One day the sergeants agreed we'd moved a rail.

We had spent an hour learning to build railroads. No theory, just how to lay track where someone else wanted it. The ties were already in place, so we didn't learn how to bed them. It was our job to lay the rails on the ties and spike them down. Coolie labor. But we weren't coolies. We couldn't do it.

The entire platoon would crowd around a single rail and heave, our hands stretched across the rail, covering the length of it so you couldn't see the steel. There wasn't enough room for all of us to squat down together, so most of us stood bent over, with our tails in the air, like sandpipers picking at a wave. There was no purchase. We might as well have been trying to lift cannonballs by palming them across the top.

We strained, and we all rose approximately together. All but the rail. We tried again, and the sweat loosened our grips. We could have been standing on the rail for all it moved.

The sergeants added their encouragement, but the rail was deaf, and there was no room for anyone else around it. And nothing changed. So the sergeants rearranged us on the principle that you can lift yourself by your own bootstraps if you just use the right sequence of jerks. But the rail knew better physics. For all we could tell, it might already have been spiked down.

The time came when our hour was up and the rail was where it had been in the beginning. We had one hour allocated to moving track, and we had used it. We had to go on to our next hour and learn how to carry timbers to a bridge. That rail had become a small crisis. We couldn't move it, and we couldn't qualify as Engineers until we did. And until we qualified as Engineers, we couldn't go to Vietnam.

The speed with which the sergeants resolved the problem suggested they had encountered it before. They agreed we had laid the rail, checked the box attesting that we had, and from then on, we had moved it.

Later, in a western, I think, I saw real coolie labor laying track. Nobody stooped. The coolies all had tools like long-handled ice tongs that grabbed the rails and let them walk upright.

26

■ FLOATING FREE

Hot afternoon in May.

We'd spent the day assembling heavy steel panels into a bridge. A giant erector set for children much bigger than we were. The sky was clear. The sun glared off the water. We were wrung out, and we still had to take the bridge apart. To put the pieces back into the box. Upstream another company was dragging pontoons down to the water. Men in green boats, roaring light and quick on the river, pushed the floats together into a bridge.

I knew then what I wanted to do in the army. I didn't know who those men in boats were or how they got to be there. But whoever they were, they didn't hump big pieces of steel. And they didn't carry packs. And the sergeants were all onshore. They were cool and free, and I ached to ride with them. Only I didn't know how to get a boat.

■ BUSTING UP

The principal view from the Appalachian Trail is the leaves you walk through.

I'd hiked the Trail when I was a kid and spent most of the time staring at those leaves. Step after step, maybe a hundred steps a minute. Five thousand an hour when you subtracted for rests. Fifty thousand a day. Some days lasted longer. And every time I took a step, I looked at the place I was about to put my foot and saw a colored bed of fallen leaves. Every glance recorded a circle of maybe twenty leaves. A quick snapshot before moving on to the next step.

At the end of the day, I'd looked at maybe a million leaves and all that night I dreamed of leaves. A great endless ribbon of leaves uncoiling behind my eyes as my brain erased their colorful images to make room for tomorrow's pictures.

We were to be Engineers, but the army never taught us anything about construction. That wouldn't be our job. As far as I could tell, our job would be to bust things up. And that's what we spent June 5 doing. Busting concrete.

Somebody had poured a slab of concrete out in the woods. It was our job to take it out. It had cured a long time and was as hard as Stone Mountain granite by the time we got to it. We spent the day chipping away at it with chisel point jackhammers. I always thought, without knowing, that in another clearing that very day, a platoon of Construction Engineer trainees was pouring another slab for another platoon of Combat Engineer trainees to bust up. A neat, closed cycle. Nothing wasted. Nothing used. We traded off on the jackhammers but were supposed to watch when we weren't actually chipping. So I spent the day looking at fragments of concrete shooting off the slab. When you counted the small stuff, it was maybe 35 fragments a second. About 125,000 an hour. By the end of the day, I had watched the jackhammer shoot off around a million fragments at violent angles.

When we were done, we marched back to the barracks and I went over to the dayroom. Someone had left the TV on and the news hadn't changed. It had only become repetitive.

28

"Sandbags and machine guns ring the capital after last night's shooting. . . .

"Roosevelt Grier was apparently uninjured as he subdued the senator's would-be assassin. I suppose the one measure of satisfaction we can take from all of this is imagining what must have gone through that gunman's mind as Rosie Grier came down on top of him. . . .

"From the senator's bedside: 'The senator continued to weaken throughout the long night and now his doctors think it is only a matter of . . .'

"The question from here, Walter, is not how Sirhan got into the service pantry under the hotel but how he knew the senator would use that service pantry to leave the ballroom. . . .

"We have not been allowed access to the senator's room, but we have obtained this diagram of his head. According to those on the scene, the bullet, or bullets, passed through the senator's skull just behind the left ear, showering bone fragments, and possibly bullet fragments, throughout the rear of his brain. His doctors say that it would be virtually impossible . . ."

The diagram was covered with dots showing where each confirmed fragment had been located. It looked more like a shot-up road sign than the outline of a human head.

"This just in. Senator Robert F. Kennedy, only yesterday triumphant in his victory in the California primary and believed by many to be the next nominee of the Democratic party for president, died about half an hour ago in Los Angeles, the victim, like his older brother, John Fitzgerald Kennedy, of an assassin's bullet."

That night a million bone fragments, thrown up by jackhammers, unreeled through my sleep.

■ PIONEER

I was running a chain saw when I found out what army Engineers really do.

"You dufous mothers. Better listen up and use them oiling buttons.

"You think you ain't going to need to know how to use a chain saw where you're going? Well, what the hell you think you going to be? PIONEERS. That's what the hell. God damn pioneers.

"You know what's the motto of the Combat Engineers? 'FIRST IN, LAST OUT,' that's what. Like the point of a dagger. Where you going ain't going to be no infantry there to wipe your butts for you you get into trouble.

"You seen those pictures of choppers dropping troops on bald hilltops over to Nam? Where you think they get them bald hilltops from? You think maybe they've got bald hilltops lying around Nam, waiting for our choppers? No. HAIL NO. Somebody went in there the day before and cut all the trees down to make a place for those GOD DAMN choppers. Somebody with chain saws. So keep them oiled. You going to need them."

All that didn't make me think about oiling the chain. It made me think about a squad of VC sitting around a jungle camp when the sound of saw motors cut through the trees:

"You hear something, Charlie?"

"Sounds like chain saws on that hill over there."

"We got any chain saws in the area?"

"Don't think so."

"Well grab your AK47, I'll fetch along the mortar. We'll go take a look."

They'd be sighting in while we were oiling the chain.

■ DEMOLITION

The Big Piney flowed through a corner of Fort Leonard Wood. A typical warm, slow Missouri river with a rocky bottom and sandy bars. We would approach the river from the flats to the west and watch it snake along the foot of a line of rough gray cliffs. Cliffs which, to midwestern eyes, looked high and rugged. Twisted oaks leaned over the tops, and lesser trees clung to the face. We were never there but five or six red-tailed hawks soared on the wind that scooped up over the bluffs.

Some places, the Big Piney brushes the foot of the cliffs. Others, such as where we sweated over the steel bridge, it sweeps near the cliffs, with a narrow wooded strip of gravel separating it from the sheer rock. At still other places it winds miles away. That is where the sergeants taught us demolition.

We marched in, river to our back, and spent the morning in a hut, staring at blocks of explosive.

"This one burns at twenty-three hundred feet per second."

"This one burns at nineteen hundred. That's why we call it a low explosion. It's made out of nitrates. Fertilizer. That's why it burns so slow. It's shit."

They trotted out some detonator cord. It looked like plastic clothesline, and you could do anything with it you could do with clothesline. Except after you tied it around something you could set it off. I could think of all sorts of uses for it.

In the late afternoon we went outside to blow things up. Confidence building, they called it. Warding off fear.

We lined up on a grassy field bordered by a rugged hardwood forest still blossoming with dogwood and redbud in the late spring, sloping down to the gleaming cliffs, beautiful in the late afternoon sun. We filed down to the dry gravel bar and set our charges at the foot of the bright rocky wall. We filed back and were a quarter of a mile away, on the shady slope, when we set off the explosives.

FIRE IN THE HOLE

Fragments from a half mile of the most beautiful scenery in Missouri filled the sky at twenty-three hundred feet per second. The hawks flapped and were gone and the bottom of those solid cliffs vanished in gray dust.

▪ CHOSEN

> There's a man goin' 'round takin' names
> There's a man goin' 'round takin' names
> Well he took my father's name and it left
>   my heart in pain
> There's a man goin' 'round takin' names

We stood in ranks in front of the orderly room while the first sergeant read down the list.

"Aldermack, Oszkar, Ninetieth Replacement Battalion, Bien Hoa, Republic of Vietnam,

"Aldrich, David W., Ninetieth Replacement Battalion, Bien Hoa, Republic of Vietnam,

"Allan, Orval R., Ninetieth Replacement Battalion, Bien Hoa, Republic of Vietnam, . . ."

We had all stood together as brothers. As our names were called, we broke into small groups, according to our destination. We were no longer brothers to those who stood elsewhere. They seemed as distant to us as the Hundred Years War.

". . . Casey, Jeremy M., Ninetieth Replacement Battalion, Bien Hoa, Republic of Vietnam,

"Chan, Lawrence, Headquarters, Sixth Army, Presidio of San Francisco, San Francisco, California,

"Colt, Sonny H., Ninetieth Replacement Battalion, Bien Hoa, Republic of Vietnam, . . ."

But most of us wound up in the same group. At the end, a quick glance wouldn't have told the difference between the new group and the one that had marched out onto the field.

". . . Dicken, George A., Ninetieth Replacement Battalion, Bien Hoa, Republic of Vietnam,

"Doornink, Douglas L., Ninetieth Replacement Battalion, Bien Hoa, Republic of Vietnam,

"Duff, Charles F., Ninetieth Replacement Battalion, Bien Hoa, Republic of Vietnam, . . ."

But the new group was a little smaller. A few people stood on other parts of the parade ground, two or three together. Others

stood alone, no one sharing their assignments, although most
would have volunteered.

". . . Fiocci, Virgil, Ninetieth Replacement Battalion, Bien Hoa, Republic of Vietnam,

"Frank, Thomas T., Twelfth Engineers, Eighth Infantry Division, Dexthelheim, Federal Republic of Germany,

"Garztecska, Dominic, Ninetieth Replacement Battalion, Bien Hoa, Republic of Vietnam, . . ."

Out of 160 people, ten or fifteen percent at the most did not go to Vietnam. Every time a name was called for somewhere else, there would be a buzz of speculation. But by and large, the people assigned elsewhere couldn't explain their good fortune, and neither could we. We could find no distinction between them and us except that they had been chosen to live, while some of us would surely die.

". . . Maldars, Raymond O., Ninetieth Replacement Battalion, Bien Hoa, Republic of Vietnam,

"Marvin, Robert E., Ninetieth Replacement Battalion, Bien Hoa, Republic of Vietnam,

"Mennestik, Francis, Ninetieth Replacement Battalion, Bien Hoa, Republic of Vietnam, . . ."

It was a Calvinist election, and there was no explaining it. Some few were chosen, and the rest of us weren't. There wasn't a damn thing any of us could do about it. Dwelling on it would make you superstitious.

> There's a man goin' 'round takin' names
> There's a man goin' 'round takin' names
> Oh, he took that liar's name, his tongue
>   got twisted and he died in shame
> There's a man goin' 'round takin' names.

All of us facing the orderly room that afternoon were civilians. We were in the army only because we could not escape it. We would not have been there if times had been different. I don't think that any of us made the army our career. Yet we were the ones who fought the war. We were the civilians who stood facing the professional soldiers who called our names.

". . . Parisi, Gayle F., Ninetieth Replacement Battalion, Bien Hoa, Republic of Vietnam,

"Parker, Allen, Second Infantry Division, Pusan, Republic of Korea,

"Pascuzzi, Anthony, Ninetieth Replacement Battalion, Bien Hoa, Republic of Vietnam, . . ."

The army was rigid with sergeants who had eighteen or nineteen or twenty years in the service who had never seen Vietnam. Soldiers whose mission was to process draftees to fight the nation's wars.

". . . Townsend, Skip, Ninetieth Replacement Battalion, Bien Hoa, Republic of Vietnam,

"Trainer, James A., Ninetieth Replacement Battalion, Bien Hoa, Republic of Vietnam,

"Unger, Nathan A., Ninetieth Replacement Battalion, Bien Hoa, Republic of Vietnam, . . ."

Civilians do this: they support an army that does not fight. An army that they send their sons to when the fighting comes. Then, when the fighting's ended, such of their sons as remain come home to pay taxes to support an army that does not fight.

". . . Yangishi, Tsutomu, Ninetieth Replacement Battalion, Bien Hoa, Republic of Vietnam,

"Yeager, Simon S., Ninetieth Replacement Battalion, Bien Hoa, Republic of Vietnam,

"Zachery, Martin, Ninetieth Replacement Battalion, Bien Hoa, Republic of Vietnam."

When they were done, the sergeants formed us up into ranks and marched us away, different groups to different places.

> There's a man goin' 'round takin' names
> There's a man goin' 'round takin' names
> Never let him catch you with your work
>   undone when he takes your name
> Never let him catch you with your work
>   undone when he takes your name
> Never let him catch you with your work undone,
>   if you do hell will be your new home
> There's a man goin' 'round takin' names.

■ GRADUATION

Fort Leonard Wood employed a marching band to play at the little ceremonies that run through the day at every army post. One morning they played for us.

We paraded around the drill field to their music and then stood in ranks in front of a bleak little reviewing stand while we were declared graduated. It all seemed very strange. I'd never thought of training as something that anybody graduated from. To me, going through training was like traveling down a pipe, a period of time to be passed through and endured. When you reached the end, you were done.

Still, that dusty little ceremony was a nice touch. Plenty of us out there that morning had never graduated from anything, and it made us feel proud of ourselves.

■ CU CHI

■ OAKLAND ARMY BASE

I flew commercial to San Francisco and then took a cab to the
Oakland Army Base. It was a minimum security prison se-
cluded behind chain link and barbed wire. It must have been
tougher to cross that fence than some of the perimeters we set up
in Vietnam. We all came to that place on our own like white-collar
criminals reporting to jail. When we left was up to the army.

A prickly hedge of demonstrators wearing flowers and peace
patches stood in our way. A girl with breasts bouncing lightly be-
neath an olive drab T-shirt tried to hand me a daisy. I didn't want it.

> If you're goin' to San Francisco,
> Be sure to wear
> Some flowers in your hair.

That driver didn't honor such picket lines and shoved on through.
A thicket of balled fists and ugly faces. Spitting and cursing. Open
hands slapping at the hood and scratching at the mirrors. I was glad
they hadn't found any bricks.

> If you're goin' to San Francisco,
> You're gonna meet
> Some gentle people there.

Inside was a sergeant.

"Get your ass on over to the orderly room, Troop."

We slept all together in an old airplane hangar. A huge building
with rows of double bunks heading for the vanishing point in every
direction. There were thousands of us. And more thousands
passed through every two or three days. A lavish tide of men
gathered for a generous purpose.

We all knew where we were going and what might happen when
we got there. But none of us resisted the going. All that went on
outside the gates. We lay at the calm center of the fire storm that
was building over the war. Our safety was given as the main reason
for backing out and our sacrifice as the chief reason for staying in.   39

Voices not our own spoke through our mouths. Opinions were pro-
nounced in our names, but our opinions were never sought.

After the busy hustle of training, Oakland was an easy time. Not
much to do but wait. We were there for combat gear and, after we
had it, to be formed into groups and put on airplanes. We carried
everything except weapons on those planes. Weapons were issued
in Vietnam. In other wars, American soldiers carried their weapons
with them. I guess nobody had worried about hijackings then.

Uniform issue: We might have been back at the reception sta-
tion. Call out your size and recoil down the counter.

"TROUSERS?"

"Long."

"TROUSERS, FATIGUE, TROPICAL ISSUE, O.D., FOUR EACH,
MOVE IT."

"SHIRT?"

"Medium."

"JACKET, FATIGUE, TROPICAL ISSUE, O.D., FOUR EACH, MOVE
IT, TROOP. . . ."

"T-SHIRT, MEDIUM, O.D., SIX EACH, MOVE IT. . . ."

"SOCKS, MEDIUM, O.D., SIX EACH . . . "

"LINER, HELMET, O.D., ONE EACH . . . TRY IT ON, TROOP. . . ."

"Boots? What about boots? We've got to . . . "

"NEXT ROOM. MOVE IT, TROOP."

Our army prides itself on its boots. The rest of the uniform can
pinch or rub, but boots have to fit. No complaints. So we picked our
own from an enormous room lined with shoe boxes, like books in a
library. We went at it, experimenting with size after size, until we
found a pair that fit every eccentricity of our individual feet. Then
we took one a half size larger all around.

"YOUR FEET'S GONNA SWELL, TROOP. IT'S GONNA BE HOT
WHERE YOU'RE GOING, AND IT'S GONNA BE EVEN HOTTER
WHERE YOU GONNA GO IF YOU FUCK UP AND GET YOURSELF
KILLED CAUSE YOU CAN'T WALK IN THEM BOOTS."

So many boots in that room. I'd never seen one of anything so
repeated. There were boots in there for the armies of the world.
Strong boots with eighth-inch steel plates in the soles and flexible
canvas uppers to let the water out.

They were boots to turn the course of history. Lee could have
beaten Grant to the Blue Ridge in those boots. Napoleon could
have gotten his armies home from Moscow.

Where had such boots come from? America snapped its fingers, signed a procurement contract, and there they were. In such a profusion we could never wear them all. Many times more boots than soldiers waiting in the hangar. More boots than all the feet that would march through the Oakland Army Base during the entire war. Boots that would wind up strewn over Southeast Asia or scattered around surplus stores for antiwar demonstrators to buy.

We should have found some way to show the enemy those boots, the offhand fruit of our productive spirit. Those boxes, all in their neat rows. The sight would have broken his heart.

And the boots were only the nearest of the great mountains of goods that had been made for us. Somewhere lay flotillas of ships filled with rifles, silos of bullets, and whole prairies paved with tanks. Everything we needed to win the war, if that war could have been won with bullets and boots and tanks. And maybe it could have if only we had wanted to win it.

Drag it back to the barracks. Nothing to do but wait.

And nap.

And sit.

And wander around. But the bunks all looked the same. Only the people looked different and they were all strangers. All going through the same thing.

And lie down.

My section was called to supper. When we got back, I wandered over to the dayroom. Television.

Viet Cong flags on television.

Viet fucking Cong flags at the Democratic convention.

Delegates inside complaining about Mayor Daley. Cops outside. Reporters with bloody heads talking to kids carrying enemy flags.

"Like it's happening all over, man. This war's wastin' our people. We gotta stop this napalm thing. It's offing our brothers, man. We're all one against this criminal fascist Amerikan pig government. All over the country. All over the planet, man . . ."

There's a whole generation
With a new explanation,
People in motion,
People in motion,
People in motion.

Cops dragged them away, the seats of their pants fluttering red, white, and blue as they went.

People in motion.

". . . with the Yippies having nominated a pig for president and every radical group in the country seeming to have converged on Chicago for the convention, the city is in chaos. Mayor Daley has sworn to keep law and order. Whether he will be able to do so remains to be seen.

"Now back to the convention floor."

". . . the state delegation chairman who was seized by the guards in the convention hall and hustled off in handcuffs."

The camera flicked to a pep rally. Crowds chanting.

"HO, HO, HO CHI MINH . . . "

". . . currently unable to interview Mayor Daley, who is jeering at Senator . . . "

"HO, HO, HO CHI MINH . . .
THE NLF IS GONNA WIN . . . "

Political chants. Ugly. Meant to outrage. And to hurt.

"This just in, Walter. Hugh Hefner is reported to have been clubbed by police outside the Hilton. No word yet as to the extent of his injuries."

"HEY, HEY, LBJ—HOW MANY KIDS DID YOU KILL
   TODAY? . . . "
"HEY, HEY, LBJ—HOW MANY KIDS DID YOU KILL
   TODAY? . . . "

"The Lou Breeze Orchestra has been instructed to strike up a lively tune in the event of prolonged demonstrations. . . ."

"HEY, HEY, LBJ—HOW MANY KIDS DID YOU KILL
   TODAY? . . . "

". . . the debate on bombing North Vietnam had just ended when the chanting began. The bombing issue is hotly felt among many, if not all of the delegates here tonight, many of whom believe the bombing is immoral and have publicly characterized it as a 'war crime.'"

"HEY, HEY, LBJ—HOW MANY KIDS DID YOU KILL TODAY?"
"HEY, HEY, LBJ—HOW MANY KIDS DID YOU KILL TODAY?"
"HEY, HEY, LBJ—HOW MANY KIDS DID YOU KILL TODAY?"

"I can see Lou now, stepping up to start the music, which will keep playing until the chanting stops."

> Off we go
> Into the wild blue yonder,
> Climbing high into the sun;
> Here they come, zooming to meet our thunder,
> At 'em boys, give 'er the gun!

"HO, HO, HO CHI MINH. HO, HO, HO CHI MINH."

> Hands of men,
> Blasted the world asunder;
> How they lived God only knew. . . .

". . . among the injured were two Bunnies who fainted when a squad of police chased about a dozen demonstrators through a glass window into the Haymarket Lounge, where they were working at the time. . . . "

It was quiet back at the barracks. Dead.
People talking softly or lying on their bunks, thinking about sleep.
At the dayroom more demonstrators were being hauled away.

". . . police, after having been pelted with hotel crockery, bags of urine, bags of fecal matter, and smoked fish, entered the hotel and broke into the McCarthy campaign suite. . . . "

Children capered over Chicago in their self-indulgent way. Cursing. Insulting. Intentionally offending. It never occurred to them that the cops might feel entitled to their own measure of self-indulgence and they were bitter when the cops took it.

". . . then a policeman asked her whether it was 'against the law, Mrs. Bubble-eyes'?"

Early the next day we were marched onto buses and driven to Travis for our flight to Vietnam. It was such a quiet ride. The Democrats were still rioting over Chicago when we left. And for two more days after that.

Happy Days Are Here Again!
The skies above are clear again.
Let us sing a song of cheer again,
Happy Days Are Here Again!

■ FLIGHT OVER

WELCOME ABOARD FLYING TIGER FLIGHT 213 TO SAIGON
WITH INTERMEDIATE STOPS IN ANCHORAGE AND TOKYO

Travis to Ton Son Nhuit. Military base to military base on a civilian plane.

FASTEN YOUR SEATBELTS SECURELY, RETURN YOUR SEAT
BACKS AND TRAY TABLES TO THEIR FULL UPRIGHT POSI-
TIONS, AND OBSERVE THE NO SMOKING SIGNS.

Every seat filled. Row on row of army green. A dark forest with
colorful stewardesses flickering along the paths.

THE FLIGHT ATTENDANTS WHO WILL BE SERVING YOU TO-
DAY ARE ANGEL, AMBER, AND DREAMA.

Seventeen hours across nine time zones to the other side of the
world. An aisle seat and nothing to do but read *Newsweek*.

ANGEL WILL NOW POINT OUT THE SAFETY FEATURES
ABOARD OUR BOEING. . . .

Politics and speculation crowded the magazine. Anesthesia at
thirty thousand feet.
Settling in for a slow flight.

Ex-President Eisenhower suffered his sixth heart attack after
watching his own taped speech at the Republican convention.

"MOTHER FUCK."
"What?"
"MOTHER FUCKING HIPPIES."
The man next to me was a child. Eighteen years old. Seventeen,
maybe. I'd never seen him before and I did not conclude I would
like to see him again.

... LOSS OF CABIN PRESSURE, THE OXYGEN MASKS
ABOVE EACH SEAT WILL DROP AUTOMATICALLY . . .

"You SEE them hippies?"
"Back at the gate?"
"Yeah. And on television."
"Couldn't miss them."
"Well, PISS on them."
I nodded and he fell back to yelling to himself.

Three days of looting, firebombing, and sniping. Six hundred
National Guardsmen. Three dead and eighteen wounded in
riots in Liberty City protesting the "lily-white" makeup of the
state delegation.

"MOTHER FUCKING SCUM. They shouldn't be allowed to LIVE.
Who the HELL do they think they are?"

Nixon's the one.

I didn't know. And I didn't care to conjecture. But he was on my
arm, and I didn't care for any fights, either.

Ron Swoboda of the Mets got into a screaming match on the
team plane with Don Cardwell. Don had warned him to "take
off those fucking love beads." Cardwell was a fashion conser-
vative. Right down to his $110 green alligator shoes.

"You think those fucking HIPPIES should be home, fucking in the
streets like mother fucking DOGS, while we're off in the Nam?"

> For those who come to San Francisco,
> Summer time will be a love-in there.
> In the streets of San Francisco,
> Gentle people with flowers in their hair.

There wasn't a graceful way to answer that.
"Course not."

Agnew lectured moderate Negroes for not doing more to con-
trol extremists.

"You God DAMN right."

Moderate Negroes accused Agnew of "guilt by pigmentary association."

"Government ought to round up those God DAMN bastards and throw away the God DAMN keys."

Hugh Hefner agreed to pay $3.7 million to settle a class action suit brought by a *Playboy* keyholder who had been issued a cardboard key.

I couldn't avoid talking for seventeen hours, but I figured I didn't have to say any more than the minimum. Short answers till he got bored. He mostly took it as agreement.

And he didn't bore easily.

"Drop that scum over North Vietnam. Let them and the North FUCKING Vietnamese figure what to make of each other. They'd learn about their peace shit mighty GOD damn quick."

"Damn quick."

"DAMN STRAIGHT. THEN let them come home. Tell their hippy scum friends what the Viet FUCKING Cong is all about."

Actually, that sounded like a pretty good idea, but I couldn't see the benefit in telling him.

"Speak from experience."

"You GOT it, buddy. Shake them bastards up. You and me, lucky to be sitting together."

"Lucky."

"One thing. When I get back to Oakland, I'm gonna rip the nuts off the first one of them mother fuckers gets near me. Then it's gonna be just me and his old lady. I'll be up her loose dress quicker'n she can cross her legs. If she puts up a fight, be just that much more fun. But I don't see it. The ones ain't sluts are all whores. Just a few slaps. That's all it'll take."

Teddy escorting Jackie to Skorpios. Didn't say why. Maybe he went along as a chaperone. Didn't say who needed chaperoning, either.

"Just a few."

"By GOD I hope we get stationed together. Be with somebody

with some God damn balls. Knows what's right, if you get what I mean."

He tapered off.

Eventually.

And started in on the soldier by the window. I didn't begrudge him the time. Seventeen hours over the Pacific. A *Newsweek*'s only good for about forty-five minutes. That's why I stopped subscribing.

Not much outside. Just bright clouds. Every now and then a stewardess would come by to fuss over us, but given our haircuts and our uniforms, I couldn't see how she could make any distinction between us. Maybe she had us listed by seat number.

Nothing to mark the passage of the hours. We could have been stuck in time, flying forever toward a lost destination. . . .

GOOD AFTERNOON, GENTLEMEN. WE HAVE JUST CROSSED THE INTERNATIONAL DATELINE. IT IS NOW 1:03 P.M. AUGUST 30, 1968.

Off United States time and onto Asia time. We'd lost a day on that flight. If we came back the other way, we'd get that day back. If we didn't, we never would. Fifty-seven thousand of us had their days cut short on the other side of that line.

I couldn't gauge what lay below the shining clouds, but I knew we had to fly along the Kuriles on the way to Japan. I wanted to see them. Russia out the window. The hidden hand we were wrestling in Vietnam. The dark power swallowing our ally and killing our soldiers. But as hard as I looked, I could see only clouds.

"I'D SURE LIKE TO PLAY CARNIVAL WITH HER. . . . "

It was my seatmate, discussing women.

"What?"

". . . the one with the jugs over there."

"You mean Amber?"

"Yeah, the one with the jugs. I sure could play carnival with her."

"Carnival?"

"Yeah. She'd sit on my face and I'd try to guess her weight."

"Oh."

"I could sure get my tongue around that, if you know what I mean."

The *Newsweek* was still in the seat pocket in front of me.

"Lots of it where we're going. Chicks got long slits in their skirts
and ain't never heard of no bra. Sort of joggle when they walk.

"One of them bends over, front or back, I'll be on her case like a
duck on a June bug. . . . "

Pictures of Julie Nixon and David Eisenhower flirting and
playing.

"Duck on a June bug."

"Yeah, that's me. I got good eyes. Twenty-twenty hindsight and
twenty-twenty foresight, if you know what I mean."

Julie on David's lap. The hem of her dress pulled up to about
her waist.

"You can have them chicks, too. A beer. A dollar. A box of C's.
Whatever you got. They'll give.

"And dope. Best God damn dope in the world. Am I ever gonna
find out about that dope."

Every now and then I shoved over him to stare down at the bank
of glaring clouds. But I never saw past them until we came in low
over Japan.

Once, while I was stretching toward the clouds shining outside, a
beautiful, fragile stewardess materialized on the arm of my seat.
Dreama, I think.

"What're you lookin' for?"

"The Kuriles. You know when they'll be out there?"

"No, but we're bound to pass them sometime. I can ask the
captain, if you want."

"I would appre——"

"What's this? What're you readin'?"

"Edie Adams, Ernie Kovacs's widow. Just had a son. Married to a
photographer now."

"Oh, I *loved* him. Watched his show every week. Went home and
cried when I read about the wreck. Just *cried*. You know that band
he had? The one with the monkey that played the banana?"

We could keep this up all the way to Saigon.

"Should have been his . . . "

"THIS GUY'S COOL. DON'T TAKE NO HIPPY SHIT. WHEN HE
GETS BACK, HE'S GONNA CLEAN THEIR ASSES."

It was my seatmate, chuckling to my insubstantial beauty.

"MOTHER FUCKING HIPPY SCUM.

"GONNA SNATCH THE BALLS OFF EVERY ONE OF THEM MOTHER FUCKERS, AND THEN HE'S GONNA LAND ON THEIR WHORE BITCH OLD LADIES. SLAP THEM AROUND A LITTLE, TOO, IF THEY NEED IT. TOLD ME SO HIMSELF JUST NOW. . . ."

Dreama had already started to get up.

". . . KNOWS HOW TO MAKE BITCHES DO . . . "

Almost everybody on the plane was looking at us. Everybody except my pretty little friend. She'd drifted across the aisle to somebody else's seat arm before my companion had finished complimenting me.

Erle Stanley Gardner married his secretary;

Gunther Sachs planned his divorce from Brigitte Bardot. She'd been linked to a twenty-four-year-old Italian night club owner. Said she was bored;

A sugar heiress died;

A Pennsylvania congressman died;

Several hundred Americans in Vietnam died, too, but their names weren't listed.

Off to sleep.

Awake and to the bathroom.

Asleep.

Awake.

Talk.

Sleep.

And finally Japan and a change of crew.

Then Vietnam out the window. No clouds there. We could see it just fine.

THE CAPTAIN HAS LIT THE FASTEN SEATBELT SIGN, INDICATING OUR INITIAL DESCENT INTO SAIGON. THE WEATHER THERE IS CLEAR AND NINETY-FOUR DEGREES. WE'LL BE ON THE GROUND IN APPROXIMATELY FOURTEEN . . .

Pale greens and silvers, bright as the clouds. All that training, and we had never been told what was there. Nothing but the names we'd heard on television. Places as romantic sounding and as deadly as any Americans had ever fought over. Names as soft and

as personal as Shiloh Church and as strange and suggestive as
Bougainville.

Outside, the Boloi Woods, the Iron Triangle, and the Black Vir-
gin Mountain slid beneath us as peacefully as the quiet fields and
friendly villages.

> Elements of the First Air Cavalry encountered stiff resistance
> in the Boloi Woods. Two dead and three wounded were re-
> ported in action near the Iron Triangle. Communist casualties
> are at least twenty-four known dead. . . .

Television doesn't teach geography very well. The maps are too
small, and they go by too quickly. Yet it burned those names into
the consciousness of a generation. Wherever we went, it would be
our solace that we could go to only one place at a time.

A bump and we were down.

> ON BEHALF OF YOUR ENTIRE FLYING TIGER CREW WE
> WOULD LIKE TO WELCOME YOU TO SAIGON. FOR YOUR
> SAFETY AND THE SAFETY OF THOSE AROUND YOU, PLEASE
> REMAIN SEATED UNTIL THE PLANE IS PARKED AT THE PAS-
> SENGER GATE AND THE ENGINES HAVE BEEN TURNED
> OFF. THE CAPTAIN WILL TURN OFF THE "FASTEN SEAT-
> BELT" SIGN AS A SIGNAL YOU MAY MOVE AROUND THE
> CABIN. PLEASE BE SURE TO CHECK AROUND YOUR SEAT
> AND OVERHEAD RACK FOR ANY CARRY-ON BAGGAGE YOU
> MAY HAVE BROUGHT ON BOARD WITH YOU.

And instant promotions. We were all PFCs. Automatic. Enlisted
men got a bump in grade when they arrived. It was a good thing,
too. I never saw another stripe over there.

> ON BEHALF OF THE CAPTAIN AND YOUR ENTIRE FLYING
> TIGER CREW WE WOULD LIKE TO THANK YOU FOR CHOOS-
> ING FLYING TIGER AND HOPE THAT WHEN YOUR SCHED-
> ULE PERMITS WE MAY HAVE THE PLEASURE OF SERVING
> YOU AGAIN. WE ALL WISH YOU AN ENJOYABLE STAY HERE
> IN SAIGON OR, IF YOU ARE CONTINUING ON, A SAFE AND
> PLEASANT TRIP TO YOUR DESTINATION.

There was a long pause while her words echoed in her mind.
Then she choked and started to cry over the PA system.

■ BUS RIDE IN

Big green buses met us at the airport. As if the army had engaged a tour service. Seats filled with double rows of green men, two by two to the back, where the odd man got the middle seat. Civilian bus lines should do so well: fill up at the first stop, nobody fumbling for change or asking directions. From San Francisco to combat, all we had to do was change seats.

A corporal drove us. He had the confident look of a hardened veteran, or so we thought, as he shoved into traffic, his black rifle holstered next to his seat. We guessed to ourselves how much he had seen and whether we would live to be like him. A few months later he seemed like just a coddled garrison troop with a soft job in a safe place.

Outside was all Vietnam. Shops crowded behind swarming sidewalks. Smokes and smells from headless animals turning on spits. Noises from motor bikes unburdened by mufflers. And people. Alert, active people. Not the elegant people of American dreams of the Orient but quick people with dusty, unreadable faces.

> People are strange
> when you're a stranger

A fragile capsule of America, barreling through the streets of Saigon, separated from the smiling faces by thin sheets of metal and heavy-gauge chicken wire stretched over the windows.

No one ever said what that wire was for. It wasn't to keep us on the bus. There was no place out there for us to go. We might as well have tried to desert a submarine.

All our memories were of peace, so the reason for the wire wasn't easy for us to guess. It was to keep grenades from rolling out of smiling crowds into unarmed laps.

We sat alone at intersections, dusty throngs collecting around us, hands reaching toward the bus. Self-possessed black eyes stared in while we glanced back. But you couldn't tell. You couldn't know then, and we never learned to understand, which of those faces were friendly and which wished the wire were gone from the windows. To us they were all hostile.

Another reason for the chicken wire came to mind. Hands that could clasp each other through an open window could swap dope for dollars quicker than a red light could change to green and a bus could lunge away. And the army wouldn't know about the exchange until it found half a dozen of its new troops sitting in back, giggling at their belt buckles.

Finally the light did change and we were off, bouncing along the worn road like an escaped railroad car, the corporal honking and cursing while cyclists and pedestrians melted to the side. As we rode deeper into the city, cyclists multiplied, crowds stiffened, and the bus slowed down until it was creeping along no faster than those back home. It was like a Gray Line tour of New Orleans, moving slowly past old buildings.

The rickety facades cluttered together with the crazy lettering and offbeat paint of the old signs and used storefronts they had been made from. Windows stood open over little counters, dozens to a block. Faces looked out, and people lounged. All sorts of things were bought and sold. We could recognize only a few of them. It was like a movie projected onto the windows of the bus.

The men wore faded loose-fitting clothes. Checked shirts and worn pants. American television always called them pajamas. But they weren't. They were just clothes.

Pajamas. As if these people never got out of bed in the morning. Well, they did. They got out of bed a damn sight earlier than we did.

Women wore about the same, most of them. Their dusty shirts and pants weren't so different from the men's. The outfits weren't attractive, but they were modest and they were cheap. Those who could, or rather those who could and thought it proper, wore shimmering high-collared dresses slit so far up the leg that they couldn't properly be said to have skirts at all but only extended loincloths. With their deep-colored cloth and lacquered bodices, those dresses were as different as they could be from what we had left on our side of the world, women dancing braless, rippling and bouncing in faded ankle-length granny gowns, nipples circling behind thin cloth.

A lot of us had just left such women. It hadn't been long for anybody. Still, the women flashing emerald and sapphire and gold outside the windows, all stiff and tight above the waist but so shimmering below, flicking pale thigh the way some birds flick a single colored feather when they fly, made every prick on the bus stand up as if it had been in prison for years.

> Women seem wicked
> when you're unwanted

We all knew that, if we could just get past the chicken wire, those women would spread for us. For love or for American cash.

The traffic thinned as we moved out of the city, jouncing along the semipaved streets. Army buses aren't sprung for comfort.

> Streets are uneven—
> when you're down,
> when you're strange.

The movies flashed faster and faster against the windows, burning up the time until the final reel was done. Then, a still of a lot outside a building so squat and graceless it could only have housed the U.S. Army.

■ HOLDING STATION

The next morning I stood at the end of a long green line of new arrivals. At the far end were two tables. When you reached the head, you went to the first vacant table, where a clerk handed you your assignment. It was a long wait.

We waited on defoliated clay, the hardest and barest earth I have ever seen. Beyond the wire, a hundred meters away, the rife greenery that came with the country twisted around us like a siege line. But here the land had been scraped and stamped and burned and probably poisoned so that nothing would grow at all. The barren place lay on the countryside like mange on the flank of a silken dog.

While we waited, a plane swept back and forth overhead, covering every inch of the place with some oily chemical we took to be mosquito spray.

We didn't know the units in Vietnam, so we couldn't tell our futures from looking in our folders, but we had all heard that sometimes, when infantry outfits were low on men, the army filled in with Engineers. And someone ahead of me had come back with a folder marked "Twenty-fifth Infantry Division."

"What's that?"

"Beats me. But I sure don't like the sound of it."

I didn't either. I was glad he'd gotten it instead of me.

I have never understood the role luck plays in my life. Thinking back, everything looks so preordained. Things seem to have happened the only way they could have happened. And sometimes I think that it's so.

Other times I think about the little things that made all the difference. The chances that tipped the balance. If it's luck, I can't see it. I can't detect the things that make a difference while they happen. Later, sometimes, I can recognize them by their consequences. But only dimly.

This line was different. A stack of folders waited on each table, and the person at the head of the line got the next folder. I knew my life rested as squarely on the folder I was to get as if my future had been typed inside. That folder would send me down paths along which I would never return.   55

When I took a place in line, I took the folder that went with that place, and my assignment and maybe the length of my life were set by the place I took. Some folders spelled death as surely as if I had been marked for extinction. Some meant that I would have an easy life in a base camp, would revel through R and R, and would swagger along the streets of Oakland when I got home. Some would let me prove myself a hero if I could and some would send me home early, horizontal in the back of a C-141, missing parts of my body or parts of my mind.

The thing was, I could always change folders. If I had had another piece of toast for breakfast, I would have shifted a few places back. What then? Would I have taken a step toward life and glory or toward a painful death in a prison camp?

Or maybe I was appointed to go where I went. Looking back, everything seems choreographed. I sometimes think that nothing could have changed what happened, not even if I had stepped out of line entirely and come back the next day. I would only have realigned myself with my destiny.

Or maybe my folder would just have followed me. At the end of the day there would have been one left over. A single folder, dropped into the stack tomorrow, ready to meet me when I appeared at the head of the line.

I couldn't tell and, not being able to tell, found myself at the head of the line exactly when my time came to be there. Or maybe it was just when I showed up.

I was waved over to the right-hand table. No ceremony, no "welcome aboard, sir." Just a folder and "move it, Troop." I might as well have been in Basic. And there it was, typed neatly on the cover: "Twenty-fifth Infantry Division."

I should have had more bacon.

■ FLIGHT TO CU CHI

W e bounced over to Cu Chi in the back of a C-123.
People feel claustrophobic flying inside metal tubes.
Civilian planes disguise their interior geometry with right
angles. Subtle squared-off seats and floors and interior partitions
make smaller planes look like buses and larger planes look like
movie theaters. The air force doesn't decorate its planes. It just
hangs webbed seats inside and lays pierced aluminum planking on
the floor. With nothing to disguise the aluminum arc of the hull
curving up and across and down the other side, the inside of an air
force plane looks like the inside of a metal cigar tube.

Flying in such a plane is an adventure. It's lifting out of Casablan-
ca in 1941 or flying around China with Theodore White.

We rolled down the strip at Ton Son Nhuit and off the end of the
known world. Rice land, all silvers and greens, flat and bright as a
mirror, fell away beneath us. The soft colors lay side by side across
the landscape in the casual, squarish patterns of a flagstone walk.

And strewn over everything were the circles. Circles covered
every paddy. Circles filled every circle. Big circles, little circles.
Interlocking circles. Clusters of circles. Chains of circles. Sprays of
circles. Circles covered the land as they cover a pond in the rain.

> Round like a circle in a spiral
> Like a wheel within a wheel
> Never ending or beginning on
> an ever-spinning reel.

I looked but I could not tell what they were, those soft circles
that covered the earth like rich lace. Then, as I stared, I knew.

BOMB CRATERS. ARTILLERY CRATERS. We'd put them there.
We Americans, raining bombs over and over again onto that rich
land. Those bombs had changed the very look of the country, but
they hadn't made any difference. After the bombers passed, the
farmers came back. They rebuilt their dikes. The government fixed
the roads. Nobody cared about the water-filled circles. The farmers
just planted over them, leaving crater walls curving above the
water. All filled to the same level.

57

Like the circles that you find
In The Windmills Of Your Mind.

It was all so festive, those soft curves and bright pastels. It didn't
seem like war at all. Still, what a mighty thing to have done, string-
ing such decorations over a foreign landscape.

Dark palms hung mirrored like black pinwheels from the banks
where yellow dusty roads cut through the wet. Small houses with
tin roofs dotted the roads like poor farmhouses or rich tobacco
barns back home. And always the circles drifted beneath our plane.

As the images unwind,
Like the circles that you find
In The Windmills Of Your Mind.

Cu Chi lay in the middle of this fertile land, a yellow raft in an
endless silver-green sea. Nothing grew there. As safe a place as an
American could find. An orderly Western foothold in a shimmering
wilderness.

Outside everything was soft and fecund. Muted colors and de-
ceptive shapes. Shapes to hide an army. Shapes not friends to
Americans.

■ WAITING ON THE AIRSTRIP

They left us on the airstrip, nobody to greet us.

THUD

We sat on our gear, waiting in the wilderness. We had fallen off the end of the world, and there was nowhere to go. Clusters of one-story buildings squatted transparent in the distance. Our gear wasn't going

THUD

anywhere until we knew where. And neither were we.

Every few seconds a commotion from somewhere in the distance broke our thoughts.

THUD

A shimmering figure, insubstantial in the heat, swam to us, dismembered by the noise. Whatever it was seemed too abstract to be real. A sort of metaphysical construct.

But when it arrived, the stripes on its arm

THUD

persuaded us to treat it like it was real.

On the way to the buildings it told us about the base and about the noise.

"Only the gun at the mess hall fire . . .

THUD

". . . around the clock. Keeps Charlie's head down and keeps you safe. Get your gear into   59 the orderly room over there. You want to get yourselves logged in so you can start the clock running on your time to go ho . . . "

THUD

Artillery at the mess hall? They hadn't told me about that when I signed up. I wondered if I'd . . .

THUD

. . . used to it.

Lovers walk along a shore and leave their
footprints in the sand.
Is the sound of distant drumming just the
fingers on your hand?

■ ASSIGNMENT

Another line to another table with another assignment. Another fulcrum point.

Old Clumsy Clifford had followed me all the way from the reception station. We were partners in the cosmic dance. Whatever assignment he got, I got it too. We toiled in the same vineyard. He stood in line ahead of me, and he got his folder while I watched.

"Delta Company."

"What do they . . . ?"

"Minesweepers—move it, Troop."

MINESWEEPERS? Clifford had divined my fate.

The only time I'd ever even seen a minesweeper was in a demonstration—a *demonstration*—when a sergeant tossed a dime out in the weeds and went looking for it with a gadget that looked like a floor buffer. We never got to touch the thing, and the sergeant never found the dime. I had no confidence in the process.

The Sixty-fifth Engineers were attached to the Twenty-fifth Division. The Sixty-fifth was where I wound up. Five companies in the Sixty-fifth—and each company had its own job. One built bridges. One built roads. One laid mines. One pulled them out. Some jobs were not as well regarded as others.

My turn. The clerk shoved me a one-way ticket to Delta Company and a short exciting career stooping in the sun next to Clumsy Clifford. The fix was so much on I was hardly paying attention to what he said.

"Echo Company."

"Echo? What? . . . Why not Delta?"

"Filled Delta up. You're going to Echo."

"What?"

"Bridges. You'll love them. Real heavy, but they don't blow up."

(So we've parted at last, eh, Cliff? I'll come see you in the hospital.)

They sent us over to the headquarters, me stepping out nicely and Clifford looking mournful.

■ IN-COUNTRY ORIENTATION

We waited on a row of folding chairs in a beat-up-looking room with a flag and a faded map.

"HON-YO . . . FEET."

And the colonel was among us, bearing the history of the Twenty-fifth Infantry. The Tropic Lightning Division, its patch a lightning bolt on a red taro leaf. It was named by a World War II Japanese general who observed in awe that "the Twenty-fifth strikes like tropic lightning." The division always took that as a compliment. At the time of the briefing, I did too. I had never seen tropic lightning. I have now. It sputters and flashes in the distance, fitful and ineffectual. I've never been clear that it does any damage. Who knows what the old Jap may have been thinking.

The colonel waved at the map, giving us a simple overview of the most complex of wars. I don't know whether he was scaling his talk to the audience or was just bearing in mind our level of attention, but I'd already gotten as much from television. Still, the names on television had turned into real places now. War places.

"The Boloi Woods . . . "

". . . the Iron Triangle . . . "

". . . Nui Bah Dinh, the Black Virgin Mountain . . . "

Jesus, the mountain with no middle. We held the land at the bottom in an iron ring, and we held the top by constant airlift. Everything in between belonged to Charlie. Like a broad red gash on a black thumb. We couldn't starve him out with our siege lines below. We couldn't blast him out with our bombs. We couldn't storm him out with our infantry. There he stood. And we could see that sore thumb from any place in Cu Chi and from most places in the division. And from up there Charlie could see us, our comings and our goings.

These were famous places. Television places. Places I'd heard about back home. Places I'd never wanted to be. I wanted some backwater neither side cared about. Instead, every place I'd ever heard of in this war was within walking distance of where I sat. The whole conflict condensed into a single division. And I was in that division. The rest of the country was the backwater.

I settled back in the folding chair and expected the colonel to

keep talking. But he didn't. He pointed out a group of French rub-
ber plantations and quit.

"HON-YO FEET."

And we were out of there.

Into the sun, watching phantoms pound the middle of Nui Bah
Dinh.

■ IN-COUNTRY TRAINING

Five days of in-country training.

Eighteen weeks in Missouri hadn't been enough.

We sat in a little amphitheater, bleachers on three sides of a square. The sergeant out front took to his work as enthusiastically as drill instructors always do, only he wore tropical fatigues and a jungle hat in place of pressed khakis and a Smokey Bear hat.

"Listen up, you menses, I only got five days to orientate you to the Nam and you'd best know how to take care of yourselfs when you step outside the wire. That's Charlie country out there. Any you raggedy-assed fucking new guys think its going to be like back on the block, go on and turn in your dog tags now. The clerk can type you all killed in action on tomorrow's morning report. Save a lot of running around later on.

"Charlie's everywhere out there. You think you gonna watch your own ass when you in the field? Ain't no way. Your buddy's gotta do that. And you gotta watch his. God help you if you let anything happen to him.

"Don't let a God damn FLY land on him. Feed him your C's if he's hungry. Carry him to safety when he's hurt. Stand his watch when he's tired. Kiss him when you go to bed at night and kiss him when you wake up in the morning. Cause you ain't NEVER gonna get home without him.

"People talk a lot of trash about Charlie. Well, let me tell you something about him. He's bad. But we're badder. They say that's his country out there. But it's our country, too. We go any GOD damn where we please, and they ain't nothin in this world Charlie can do about it."

There's nothing you can know that isn't known
Nothing you can see that isn't shown.
Nowhere you can go that isn't where you're meant to be . . .

"We got artillery. Every meter of this Viet FUCKING Nam is gridded in. Long as you know where you're at, we can drop shells on Charlie's head till they ain't nothing left but new dirt. His buddies won't even have to bury him.

64

"Somethin else we got. We got air strikes Charlie can't do a GOD damn thing about. Them Cobras come around the trees. Shee-it. They don't need to go over. But when they get to moving, they's faster than that bitch you left back on the street.

"And if you ever see an AC-47 with three open doors circling overhead, get down on your knees, cause nothing on this earth gonna save you now. They got miniguns back of them doors. Six-barreled 120mm gattling guns on each mount. Six thousand rounds per minute. Fires so fast the belts can't keep up, so they rotate the barrels. That son of a bitch can punctuate an entire battalion of Charlies faster than they can fall down their rat holes.

"And even if they do, a B-52'll open a tunnel thirty feet under-ground. Come over so high nobody can see it. Charlie don't know it's there until those big bombs come screaming down on top of him. Then he got no place to go but to hell.

"You don't know jack shit about fighting Charlie now, but five days from now you'll know enough to get started. Then when you're out in the field, pay attention. Those of you live through the first few weeks, you'll get the hang of it."

There's nothing you can do that can't be done
Nothing you can sing that can't be sung.
Nothing you can say but you can learn how to play the game . . .

"But any you troops think you gonna hang back, way you did in AIT, let somebody else pull the work, you ain't never goin home. You ain't never gonna see that street again.

"Only way you gonna be on that freedom bird next year is to shoot your way on it.

"Only way out of the Nam you gotta shoot your way out.

"YOU HEAR ME?"

"YES, SERGEANT."

"SHOOT YOUR WAY HOME."

> All you need is love
> All you need is love
> All you need is love,
> Love,
> Love is all you need.

"YOU MENSES HEAR ME?"

"YES, SERGEANT."

■ RIFLE RANGE

L ate afternoon on the fourth day, we went to the rifle range. It was a long walk from the place where we had been training. Clear across post.

We didn't go in formation. Nobody marched in Vietnam. Didn't want to bunch up. Better to be spread out if we were ambushed. Nobody expected to be ambushed inside the post, but since we were being trained, we walked. Like we were on patrol. Practicing to be the way we had been when we came into the army.

Along a gravel road past barracks I did not recognize. Past the mess hall. Past motor pools and past rows of half-built buildings. Happy Construction Engineers hammering in the sun. They never left post. Nobody had told me about them when I enlisted. Still, swinging a hammer on a hot roof all day might make you volunteer for the infantry. Past the EM Club and the PX and finally to a gate. A small gate, like the back door to a castle. Not really a fighting gate. More of a place to bolt through if everything turned to shit.

That gate wasn't used much. It was rusty and weeds grew around it. But it commanded a lot of enemy territory. Plowed ground sloped away from post for a couple of hundred meters, then flattened out for maybe half a klick and ended in a stand of dark trees. Charlie was good, but he'd have to be better than good to cross that.

We went out, one by one to our left, walking Indian file maybe five meters in front of the wire. There was a trail there, clusters of tall weeds on both sides. We had gone maybe half a klick when the sergeant had us stop and face out over the plowed earth we had seen from the gate. We stood there like a long picket line called up from the past. Then he had the first twenty men kneel.

"LOCK AND LOAD."

No targets out there, so there wasn't much purpose in aiming. Besides, the army supposed we could already shoot. The purpose of the exercise was to familiarize us with our M16s. We might need them someday.

"FIRE WHEN READY."

A ragged volley, a rattle of musketry from a distant war, skipped down toward the trees.

As it turned out, that was as much firing as there was to do that day. The rest of us had to learn our weapons by association.

"CEASE FIRE."

"HON-YO FEET."

They were halfway up when one green tracer spat back from the field.

A GREEN TRACER.

And slammed between two of them. A brilliant streak in the gathering dark.

"DOWNDOWNDOWNDOWNDOWNHITTHEDIRT."

An enemy tracer, and we were lined up like bears in a shooting gallery.

And then we were boring into the ground, hiding behind thin clumps of weeds. Pinned down by enemy fire while someone at the end of the line slipped back through the gate for help.

After a while help came.

A by God air strike.

A Cobra chattering over that plowed field like a swarm of venomous insects, harrowing the ground out front. Planting seeds of death.

Under cover of that mad attack we scurried, one at a time, back through the gate. Mice into a wall.

The thing I've never made sense of is why that sniper fired in the first place. Maybe he just panicked. There he was, camouflaged, waiting for dark, when all the rifles in the world opened up on him. On command. Like an execution. Hasty, scrambling for cover, he snatched up his weapon by the trigger.

Or maybe he was just very brave and thought he would get off a couple of rounds before he died.

Or maybe he was brave and unlucky. He thought he would squeeze off a round or two and slip away, but when he fired a tracer came out and the game was up.

Or maybe he was trying to infiltrate the base and didn't know about the rifle range. Then 250 men marched out, turned and began shooting at him. Basic small army tactic: fire back, it keeps their heads down. And it did. All 250 of them.

As we bundled away from that place, we could still hear the Cobra raking the plowed earth, gunning for the enemy, swooping up and down that empty field, its guns clattering like gravel spilling down a chute. For all I know, it may be there yet, turning over the poisoned earth.

■ GARBAGE

Before I drew a permanent work assignment, I just did what was available. Anywhere else it would have been KP, but KP wasn't available in Vietnam. It was too desirable. People volunteered for it. For a year of straight KP. It kept them indoors and on post. Their replacements lined up months in advance.

Garbage detail was available, and I got that. Garbage trucks left post, and so nobody wanted to be on them. A big, drab dump truck met three of us back of the mess hall. Rows of fluted cans, like those back home, were filled with breakfast.

Fried eggs nobody ate, reproachful like the eyes of starving children. Stacked shingles of still warm french toast. Brown-striped ribbons of bacon. Milk and juice and coffee grounds mixed with butter and floating in brown syrup.

We lifted the first cans, and eggs spilled over the truck like herring from a net. Then juice, butter and syrup, bacon and toast, and finally coffee grounds dumped in for traction. Food splashed to our knees.

Other cans held last night's chicken bones, weighted with meat, racks of rolls that had never reached the table, tanks of gravy, round cardboard ice cream containers as big as concrete pilings, old lard cans, empty butter boxes, enough paper to keep the Government Printing Office in business for weeks, and more coffee grounds—always coffee grounds. As if the war wasn't enough to keep us awake.

Next stop, ashes. From bullet boxes. The packaging of the stuff of war. We went to the place where people loaded magazines for M16s. We never saw the bullets, just the ashes of the boxes they came in. Somewhere yesterday's magazines were stacked like paperbacks in a used book store.

The loading was done by permanent volunteers like the guys on KP. I wondered which job was worse.

Mountains of ashes improved our footing and turned the food to filth. Food that had been harvested, assembled, processed, packaged, shipped across an ocean, stored, opened, cooked, served, ignored, thrown away, and dumped into our truck. Batteries of chickens had hatched, lived, and died just to become garbage in that truck. Families of Mexicans had stooped in the sun so we could have food sliding around under our feet. Strong young steers had their heads crushed in stockyards so we could wade in their butchered flesh.

On the day it was harvested, that food was good. While it had waited in the garbage cans it had still been good, and that country was filled with people who would have eaten it then gladly if only our wire hadn't kept them away. It had still been edible when it first lay in the truck. But the bullet boxes had ended that. Nobody was so hungry that he could eat it then. Gray filth disgraced our truck.

We could have gone the other way around the compound. If we had concluded our rounds at the mess hall, the food would have been on the top of the pile. We would have slid a good breakfast— riding a load of trash—to people who now starved.

Next came the club. The EM Club.

Barrels of beer cans. Bags of beer cans. Boxes of beer cans and loose pull tabs shining in the sun like silvery fish scales around a cleaning table.

Then the other club. The Officers' Club.

Cans. Glass: busted liquor bottles. I was never invited into that club, so I didn't know how the bottles broke, or if they were broken every night. I like to think the officers got into fights and threw things, but more likely some sergeant just thought broken glass was the army way. More poison to add to the food.

The PX.

More ashes. More burned boxes. Camera boxes, radio boxes. Stereo boxes. Record boxes. Boxes of toys that doomed men played with between patrols. The PX took the place of whores on post, and it was more profitable for the people back home.

And another club. The NCO Club.

They had glass! I'd never known you could get promoted out of beer. All those sergeants in there, drinking liquor and acting like officers.

We processed our refuse until it was worthless. Glass and metal and ashes. It could have been a load of industrial waste for all the benefit left in it.

And the whole time we were collecting it, all over camp, people were making more, turning sweet, good food and cleverly made products into filth to be hauled away.

The gate swung back, and we rolled out of Cu Chi. My first visit with the citizens of South Vietnam. I bring you garbage. Down a long slope and then over a ridge and into an enormous wasteland. We might have been driving through an open pit mine, everything was so barren. A sloping depression partly filled by an unmanaged dump. No layers of clean fill. No restrictions. Just drive in and dump what you have. Floppy papers tumbling across the gray landscape. Melted and broken glass stabbing up through rain-packed ashes. The end of the line for the extravagant productivity of a lavish nation. It could have been Herculaneum.

And yet the place supported life. Half a dozen Vietnamese stood on the crest of the ridge with a table and an ice chest and some bottles. They grinned and held up drinks. It was a concession stand.

"Hey, Joe, you want Coke? Numbah one good drink, no?"

"You no want Coke, we got many other drink. We got Budweiser. You like Budweiser? Very cold. You like. You see."

Too many stories about battery acid to go buying drinks out here. As it turned out, I didn't have a choice. The truck never slowed.

We may not have looked promising, but we were the only Americans around. The entrepreneurs broke into a run behind us, waving bottles.

"You like U.S. whiskey? We got very cheap. Jack Daniels, number one. You like. Buy Jack Daniels. Buy Coke. Make whiskey Coke. You like. You see."

"Where the hell'd he get Jack Daniels?"

"Maybe found an empty bottle in the dump."

"Looks to me like all our bottles come out busted."

"Maybe he assembled one from the parts. Got a lot of time sitting at that table up there."

"HEY. We no want drink. You bick. NO WANT DRINK. Drink number TEN. YOU BICK?"

They mostly bicked. They slowed to a trot and then turned around. All but one girl, who kept coming. By now the truck was hub deep in burned and broken things. We stood aside while the bed tilted up, and the useless filth slid out. Then the truck wasn't so dirty. The bed wasn't back down before the dirty fifteen-year-old, split off from the drink people, was upon us.

"HEY. JOE. My name Nhan. You like me. I very, very good. Numbah one hot pussy. You want fuck? My ass like machine. You have numbah one good time. I come. You see."

"No. I no want fuck."

"Gook chicks can't come. Anybody'll tell you that."

"Tough way to earn a living. Not many trucks through here in a day."

> Lady Madonna,
> Children at your feet,
> Wonder how you manage to
> make ends meet.

"BLOW JOB? I got best mouth all around. Look teeth. Best teeth you ever come across. Come on, Joe. Blow job very, very cheap. You like. You see."

> Who finds the money
> When you pay the rent,
> Did you think that money was
> heaven sent?

"NO. NO BLOW. YOU BICK? NO BLOW."

"Eat then. I crazy for eat."

"DAMN BITCH. Let go my nuts before I blow your nasty yellow ass away. YOU BICK?"

"Cut her some slack, man. She's got a papasan and two babysans to feed."

> Lady Madonna,
> Baby at your breast,
> Wonder how you manage to
> Feed the rest.

"Well, she ought to watch where she grabs. Something like that could put a guy off fucking for weeks."

When the bed was finally down, the truck churned off through the garbage, tires splashing the girl who ran along behind us, her voice cracked and shrill as a mamasan's.

"Why you no like? You want boy? You wait. I have brother here one-two minute. You like. Tightest asshole all around. YOU WAIT.

"AH, come on, Joe."

■ SHOWER

Back at camp we hosed off the truck and went for a shower. Large water tanks, heated by the sun, perched on standard army communal shower stalls. The cutting edge of practical solar technology.

Inside, the four of us, lathered and washing Vietnam from our bodies. Nothing but the sounds of bubbles crackling in our ears. Almost.

"Please . . . , please."

Crackle . . . hissssss . . . crackle . . . Like trying to listen to a radio at night.

Crackle . . . "Please . . . "

"So why don't you give him a hand?"

That sounded enough like a command that I rinsed off some soap and looked around. Nothing. Only the sort of splatting noise a frog makes on linoleum. Then

"Please . . . , please."

I looked down at the shortest Vietnamese I had ever seen. Also the most muscular. He was leaping like a salmon for the shower handle he was too short to reach.

I turned the water on, but how would he ever get it off? If somebody didn't do that for him, it would all run out of the tank.

■ THE WATCHES OF THE NIGHT

THE WATCHES OF THE NIGHT

After we ate, they led us out to the bunker line. Through the double rows of mosquito-netted hooches, past the big Chinooks, almost to the wire.

Every one hundred meters or so, all along the perimeter, the soft shapes of squat sandbag structures sat half buried in the hard soil. Dirty, rounded things partly dissolved in the tropical rains.

The army hadn't shown us any bunkers back in Missouri, so I wasn't clear what to expect. But I had images: expensive machinery. Gleaming gun barrels. Racks of shells. Smells of grease. But no.

You had to step down about three feet to get in. Nothing wet could run out, but plenty dripped down with you. The smell of stale piss shrouded the place like an aura.

Inside the stinks of puke and old beer burned like tear gas. Three soldiers in a space too small to be an oven. The other two were down there ahead of me. I could make out one crammed on a shelf against the sandbags, his knees pulled up like a Mexican idol's. The other dangled catty-cornered in a canvas hammock strung from tangled plastic clothesline. Their dark eyes glittered somewhere between derelict and Indian fighter.

The place was awash in ordnance. Fragmentation grenades, concussion grenades, phosphorous grenades, smoke grenades, rifle grenades, flares, TNT bombs, and claymores were scattered over the floor like stones on a rocky shelf. Rockets lay against the walls like the bamboos on the sides of lean-tos. Dull magazines were stacked like dominoes, and machine-gun belts hung about like dirty laundry.

"Damn, Sam. If either of you guys smoke, we're in one heap of shit."

"That's what I keep trying to tell old Raymond up there. But you can't never tell a smoker that it's no good for him."

Raymond rolled over in the hammock. The few teeth he had didn't mate up, top to bottom, so even though he could clamp his   73 jaw down farther than most, he couldn't make much progress on solid food.

He had a cigar in his mouth, but it wasn't lit. He just chewed while he talked, the cigar flicking up and down while he elaborated an aesthetic of smoking.

"The main thing is, though, you boys benefit. Drive some of this stale air out and refresh us all."

A match flared, and Raymond swallowed blue smoke. I was calculating trajectories to the door. The guy on the shelf had an opinion, too.

"I once rescued a water buffalo that broke through a latrine, so I can't say this is the foulest place I've ever been, but that cigar sure seems at home here."

"Yeah, and what about all that stuff on the floor?"

I should have known not to make suggestions around Raymond. A lazy cascade of orange sparks spilled over the side of his hammock and danced onto a pile of rocket-propelled grenades. I almost choked on my scrotum.

"I know what you mean. I've been trying to tell Ray about that shit on the floor."

Ray stuck the cigar back in his mouth so he could talk. "That shit down there got nothing to do with me. It's to protect them choppers back of us. If we ever get overrun, the first Charlie here's gonna drop a fat Chinese grenade through that gun slit. Now, them grenades don't explode with regularity, but they explode often enough so you've got to take notice of them. If the first one don't go off, he'll drop another one in here. After a while the law of averages says one of them mother fuckers gotta go off. Then, WHAMMO, the floor is gonna go off, too. And most of the walls. There's gonna be shrapnel, and fire and colored smoke and phosphorous flying around this place like Tet come on Fourth of July. And when they stop, there's not gonna be no bunker here no more. Just a big hole between number twenty-six over to the right and number twenty-eight off on the left. And one hell of a big gap in that human wave headed for the choppers."

"That's what he says," said the voice on the shelf, "but when that cigar sets that shit off, he's gonna be in the worst spot of all of us. All we gotta worry about is smoke and frags and shit. He's gonna fall, man. That shit on the floor ain't gonna blow without his hammock goin with it. That det cord he's got it strung up with burns at twenty-one hundred feet per second. No way he's gonna get out of that hammock so quick. Not only is he gonna be dodging frags, man. He's gonna fall down and wrench his back."

"That's det cord?"

"You ever try to buy clothesline over here? Careful you don't slip on those rifle grenades. They're slicker than a jar of spilled BBs."

With him on the shelf and Ray on the hammock, the only place left for me was looking out the gun slit.

THE WATCHES OF THE NIGHT

Raymond kicked a bulky cylinder leaning against the wall. The guy on the shelf looked up.

"Starlight scope. Turns things green, but once you get the hang of it, it'll pick out the little yellow fellows just fine. . . . Long as you're sitting there, why don't you take this watch with Ray?"

"Why don't I take the next one? Ray can have this one for himself."

"Can't do it. Got to be two of us."

"You mean we gotta do this together? We'll be up most of the night."

"Regulations. Two men awake all the time."

"We'll get only four hours' sleep. I hauled garbage all over the country today."

"You think we don't work? We pull these watches almost every night. The nights we don't we're in the club. Don't sleep there neither."

"Nobody can live like that."

"Can't help it. Guy that made the rules don't pull the watches.

"You pull yours down by the slit. Ray'll pull his up in the hammock. Don't have to watch so hard from up there. I'll sleep back here on the shelf. In two hours Ray'll move to the slit and guard, I'll move to the hammock and look out, and you can sleep on the shelf. We'll rotate.

"Two men on guard all the time. But with that time in the hammock you won't need so much sleep tomorrow.

"You can take the first watch from up on top. It's cooler up there, and maybe Ray'll take that turd he's been suckin up with him."

Raymond considered his cigar. "Besides the fact that I owe it to you troopies to keep this place fumigated, it's not safe to smoke out there."

He put it out, and we climbed on top of the bunker and sat with our feet hanging over the edge.

"You only smoke inside?"

"Don't want to take no chances. Climb back out here tomorrow. There's a brown spot on a sandbag about a meter in back of you. It's where Sawyer rocked back. He was sitting just about where you are. Lit up a J, and an AK47 round came out of that village over there quicker than he could cover the glow. Hit just inside his cheek. Wasn't wearing a helmet, so the back of his skull sprayed over on the grass. He snapped back and the exit hole just fit around the curve of that sandbag. Big enough to shove in a grenade and have room left to pull the pin. Pumped his blood and his brains into the sand before I could get down to the phone.

"I wouldn't be sitting anymore where you're sitting tonight. They've got that spot sighted in."

"Yeah, well, how long they keep a place sighted in?"

"Don't know but probably a while. Just happened Thursday. That's why you're here."

THE WATCHES OF THE NIGHT

After a while we went back down. I sat at the slit again.

That scope really did brighten things up. Not daylight bright, as advertised, but as bright as the bottom of a shallow lake. Greenish yellow light flashing over a blurry landscape, murky images swimming in the distance.

Those scopes were a bragging point of American technology. The army had one in every bunker. It claimed only three had ever fallen into enemy hands. Which is to say that the scopes were more carefully accounted for than soldiers.

Still, I never learned to love them. Every glance through one was a strain. They were as repulsive to the human eye as a flickering TV screen.

They were the dead end of a technical culture—a little too advanced to build right. And so expensive we worried more about them than about fighting. Only the enemy didn't care about them. Good night vision and a sense of smell were their match. Charlie couldn't light up the landscape, but he could find our bunkers at night, and that was enough.

He gridded his mortars during the day. Just like we did.

Even the first watch passes slowly. I rested my head on a sandbag to steady the scope and closed my eyes to clear my vision. Then Ray was shaking my elbow and I was choking on cigar smoke. The place stank.

THE WATCHES OF THE NIGHT

Every couple of hours we got up and moved. By the time we were done, the sleep we got was more like ten hours than four. I was propped in the window when the sun began to rise behind the bunker, washing out the shifting green of the scope with the real greens of the land.

The ground sloped down slightly from the bunker. Little tufts of grass no more than knee-high separated by patches of bare earth. Toward the bottom of the hill lay the junkyard of our concertina wire, coiled rustily along our front and strung with mines and flares and listening devices. Claymores poked out of the earth like tiny billboards advertising death to trespassers.

Farther out the land sloped gently back up, giving us a broadside view of enemy troops tiptoeing toward us.

Off to the right and back from the crest of the hill lay the hooches of the village, bright in the morning sun. Half a klick away. A long way for a sniper round. But possible if you took your time and sandbagged in first. And if you didn't have any interference, of course.

That was all I could see, out to the front. The slit didn't open to the sides or rear. What could we do when the enemy was among us?

During the night a tank had moved up behind us. They were all up and down the line. Nobody for tanks to fight, so the army just drove them to the perimeter at night. Expensive bunkers. Sandbags would have worked better. And been cheaper.

I've never liked C rations. I liked them even less that morning. The greasy taste blended too well with the ambience of the place.

Eat and talk.

"When do we get out of here?"

"When the day shift comes."

"They got daytime bunker guards?"

"Uncle Sam's got an investment in this place. You think he don't watch the wire during the daytime? Some guys' got it as permanent duty."

"I'd rather be on patrol."

"They've been on patrol. They'd rather be in a bunker."

The day shift operated on a different schedule from ours. It took its own time about getting there, but still, I didn't have any place I wanted to go.

From the top of the bunker we could see the main supply route. The MSR ran through the back gate, just on the other side of number twenty-six. The gate swung open, and a line of APCs—armored personnel carriers—slid out like boxes on a string. They were covered with American soldiers looking for the enemy. Because of the mines, they said, they rode on the outside. But I think it was more than that. I think it was their spirit. Too proud to huddle inside, carried to war in the baggage compartment.

■ PAINTING MOTTOES

Frank Halys looked at his collar a lot. He'd been a sergeant ten days. Before that he had been a corporal eleven years. He made sergeant when his plane landed at Ton Son Nhuit. Promoted like everybody else. Rumor was he had volunteered just to get the stripe. He was touchy about it.

He carried a stencil. I had a bucket of white paint and a brush.

The captain had sent us to paint "FIRST IN—LAST OUT," with a little picture of a dagger in the middle, on every vehicle in the motor pool. A bewildering sea of vehicles crowded together like cars on a factory lot. Tanks. Road-building equipment. Dump trucks. Deuce-and-a-halfs. Jeeps. Cranes. Five-tons, each with a Bailey bridge stacked in pieces on its bed. APCs. Mobile scissor bridges mounted on tank chassis. And a lot of things that I couldn't name at the time and can't remember now. Two hundred of them. Maybe two hundred and fifty. Each got a motto. Some, like the trucks, got two, so they looked like delivery vans with a name on each door.

I never really met our captain, but I caught glimpses of him in the darkness at reveille, standing erect in front of his short row of troops. With his crew cut and bloused fatigues, he looked like he was still trying to graduate from OCS.

A few weeks before, he'd had someone paint the motto of the Corps of Engineers, FIRST IN—LAST OUT, beneath the windshield of his jeep and had parked the jeep at a staff meeting where the colonel would be sure to see it.

"Good, Captain. Damn good. Point of the dagger. What being an engineering soldier is all about. I'll have that painted on all our vehicles. Show the men some spirit, by God."

The captain blushed modestly and volunteered to do it himself, meaning that Halys and I would do it. But the way it worked out, only I did it.

I stood in the tropical sun and painted while Sergeant Halys sat in the shade and made suggestions. I did all the painting, and he did all   79 the suggesting. A fifty percent administrative burden was low for that war.

It was a good job. Kept me out of the field. Regular hours. Steady pay. I worked at my own speed. Taken in context, it wasn't at all bad.

■ A MAD MINUTE

THE WATCHES OF THE NIGHT

I sat staring out the gun slit, watching the sun move down the trees and dozing to the sound of bells. They quit when the guy on the shelf answered the phone.

"Two minutes. We'll be there."

He hung up. "Lock and load, Troopies. Two minutes."

Raymond swung down from his hammock and skated on white phosphorous grenades over to where he'd left his rifle. We weren't supposed to fire them on automatic, but his switch was full over. The guy on the shelf had set up an M60 machine gun and laid the belt across the front of the gun slit. The two peered out while I was trying to figure out what was going on. I wasn't even sure where I'd left my rifle.

"So load up, buddy. Lock and load. It starts in a few seconds."

"What starts?"

"One Mad Min . . . " And they were off.

TOT . . . TOT . . . TOT . . .
tot . . . tot . . . tot . . . tot . . .   TOT . . . TOT . . . TOT . . .
TOT . . . TOT . . . TOT . . . TOT . . . TOTot . . . tot . . .
tot . . . TOT . . . tot . . .   TOT . . . TOT . . . TOT . . . TOT
                    . . . TOT . . . TOT . . . TOT . . . tot . . .   totTO
TotTOTotTOTtottot.

Firing all up and down the line. I never saw a target, only red tracers streaking into the pale night. I dug out my rifle, slapped a magazine into place, and rolled over to the gun slit.

Whatever was coming, I was there to stop it. I squeezed off a few warning rounds on semi and then switched over to full automatic. I'd never fired a weapon full like that before, and it was more fun than Christmas. But it sure used up the ammo. I spent more time locking and loading than firing. But how I did shoot.

tot . . . tot . . . tot . . . tot . . . tot . . . tot . . .
tot . . . tot.

And reload and shoot

tot . . . tot . . . tot . . . tot . . . tot . . . tot . . .
tot . . . tot.

And reload. It was better than a box of firecrackers.

"Stop. Minute's up. Hold it. HOLD IT, GODDAMN IT, cease fire."

We must have won, because all down the line you could hear the bunkers holding fire.

TOT . . . TOT . . . tot . . . tot   tot . . . tot . . .
tot . . . tot . . . tot . . . tot . . . tot.

tot . . . tot

The shooting stopped. The guy on the shelf laid his machine gun aside to cool. The smell of hot brass cut through the other smells. The odors were starting to add up like graffiti in a bus station bathroom.

"Shit, man, you didn't get much off, did you?"

"Off at what? What are we shooting at?"

"What are we shooting at? You believe this fucking new guy? What were we shooting at? We weren't shooting at nothing. It was a Mad Minute. One Mad Minute. They give us one every day. You'd been on time last night, you'd of known. Hells bells, Troopie. They don't never let us shoot at Charlie. So one minute, every day, they just let us shoot.

"We're supposed to be clearing our weapons. But don't take all that to clear no weapons. The first round is to clear the weapons. The rest is to clear us. It works too, don't it?"

It did, but it was expensive therapy. It would have been cheaper to fly over a squad of New York shrinks for the duration. But probably not as effective.

■ RHAPSODY IN BLUE

Phantoms stooped in the transparent sky, powering in toward Nui Bah Dinh, their jets screaming. First one and then the other grazed the blue side of the dark mountain and angled aloft, still accelerating. Behind they left the flash of their bombs. Over the mountain the planes fountained to the side, one to the right, one to the left, and roared down to meet at the target and rush again up opposite sides to come together over the peak and plunge tandem back onto the enemy, engines shrieking. Rockets spewed from the lead plane as it cut into the sky. Other rockets streaked below as the second plane followed it into the climb and into another dive.

Slow Saturday afternoon.

Back home we'd be drinking beer and watching the first college game of the new season. Here I was, painting mottoes.

Just another working day. So was Sunday, for that matter. But still, nobody forgot what day it was, and nobody worked any harder than he had to on Saturday.

From where I stood on an APC, stretching to paint the boom of a crane, I could see most of camp. But I couldn't see anybody working. Even the motor pool crew was gone. Sergeant Halys wasn't doing anything at all, sprawled in the shadow of a tank.

The war turned down to slow. The Phantoms were silent at that distance, though they woke the heart. Even on a slow Saturday afternoon, looping and curling around that mountain, they were a thing for the Blue Angels to study. Speed and power and precision machines. What America does. And America was very good at what it did. As good as was the enemy at stealth and murder and lies.

Pilots die on bombing runs, flying down enemy gunsights. Those two aviators came in time and again on waiting guns. They did it because they could do it and, in doing it, stick their thumbs in Charlie's slanted eye, carrying fire and steel to the dirty places and infected warrens where he hid. As long as they could do such a thing, he was no more than a scurrying creature that scuttled about at night. He was not the lord of the country. Not even the part of the country he controlled.

83

■ 84
Cu
Chi

Those joyous young aviators could have laid their bombs and their rockets in straight runs. But it was their delight to soar and swoop and glory in their precision and their power. Let dying eyes carry with them to Hell the vision of triumphant Americans laughing in the sky. Let living ears tremble at the memory of the thunder. And let our friends exult in our might.

■ OLD JOSEPH FROM CHITOWN

THE WATCHES OF THE NIGHT

After dark it was cooler outside the bunker than inside. So we sat on top with our faces to the wire and our feet pointing to the lights of the village that shot old Sawyer.

"You guys ever been to that village?"

"Yeah, once," the guy on the shelf volunteered. "Don't have much ambition to go back."

"What's it like?"

"Hot. They got my buddy there. Old Joseph from Chitown. A Chinese fifty-one-caliber machine gun tore into him. Spilled out parts I never wanted to see. That's something they're not supposed to use. Those big machine guns are only for aircraft. Course we got our fifty calibers, so I guess it comes out even.

"We were coming back from patrol—just up the road there—when they cut Old Joseph down. The rest of us dove into the ditches. He was stuck out on the road, screaming and begging. Nobody could get near him. Every time we moved, those bullets would graze the asphalt and we couldn't do nothing but dig in deeper. We were there forever, listening to the rain and Old Joseph.

"We were too close into the machine gun to call for artillery. So we just lay there. I finally knocked it out with a rifle grenade, and I was the first one up to take a look. Nobody else saw her good. Just barely thirteen. Maybe only twelve. Her shirt was ripped open, and rain was running down her tits. No bigger than pencil erasers. She was still alive then and begging for help the same way Old Joseph had. When I was done with her, there weren't any tits left or much of anything else. I got me a bronze star out of it. If I'd had it with me then I'd have jammed it up her hairless fucking cunt.

"We don't draft girls. Too weak. But strength don't mean shit. A girl like Eraser Tits can run a machine gun or a tank or a plane, for that matter, and stop an entire platoon of grunts dead in the road. And I'll tell you something else. A proper-brought-up teenage girl is as fanatical an adversary as you will ever meet. . . .

"Village is all pacified now. The government has de-fined it as 85 friendly. Just means nobody will shoot you from it in the daytime. Ain't a place in this country you want to be after dark.

"So now we leave that village alone. During the day, it's just as if they was on our side. What they do at night's their own business.

"Killed Old Joseph, and there ain't nothing the army will do about it. But there's one thing sure as hell I can do. Took all the tracers out of the belt to my M60 so nobody can see where I'm firing. Then, come the Mad Minute, I hold me a little memorial service for Old Joseph. Except this time the bullets're flying toward the village.

"They know about what time of day I'll open up, but they never know when I'm on the line. Keeps them honest."

■ REPAINTING MOTTOES

Sergeant Halys wouldn't tell me where the paint came from. It was his job to get it. Mine was to put it on where he said. Everybody needs a purpose.

Sometimes I worried about finishing. Running out of work. There wasn't any turnover in those vehicles. Once painted, they just sat there. The war never got to them, and they never had to be replaced. When the last motto was painted, I would be out of a job. And probably out in the field.

As it turned out, I didn't even come close to finishing. All that painting, but nothing ever seemed to get painted.

You can't tell one army truck from another, but you can suspect. And I was beginning to suspect I had déjà vu. I first noticed it while painting the back of a dump truck. The dents and chips in the paint and the spidery crack in the window looked familiar. A couple of mornings later I painted those dents and chips a third time and it seemed to me I was painting on top of the only fresh paint on the entire truck.

We had only three tanks in the battalion, but I painted that motto on seven tank barrels over the weeks. And on the blade of the road grader. And on the door of a deuce-and-a-half. No matter how many vehicles I'd paint, there'd be only two or three in there the next morning with mottoes. I've never been superstitious, but I couldn't explain that. Divine intervention in my favor. It made me pause.

Or maybe there was another Sergeant Halys in charge of another painting detail assigned to go out at night and paint over the white letters.

Whatever, it was a stable system. I could keep painting for as long as the paint held out, and there didn't seem to be any end to the paint. Let the war roar all around. I had found my place amid the peace and the paint.

■ BOARDWALKS IN THE MUD

THE WATCHES OF THE NIGHT

I wasn't expecting rain, but the weather didn't consult my expectations. Water soaked in. Cu Chi turned to a sticky mud that could suck the treads off a tank. Several monsoons ago, someone, who was back home watching it all on television now, had laid thousands of meters of wooden sidewalk around the camp, making the place look like Dodge City. By the time I got there, you could go wherever you wanted, walking in the rain a few inches above camp. Or you could dodge vehicles and take the gravel roads.

Painting mottoes was a chore not suited for rain, so in bad weather we moved a few vehicles into a shed, and when we had finished there, we were done. We headed home, ducking raindrops. Sergeant Halys veered off toward the NCO Club. He didn't have much cleaning up to do.

I was aimed for the shower when I came upon a soldier in brown. A shade toiling in a flooded ditch, he flung a load of watery mud to the side and then hunched back down. For every shovel of thin mud he pulled from the bottom, the sides slid in to fill the gap. He was an unbroken, glistening brown from the top of his head to the place where his body met the water.

Here was one of the damned struggling against an unending task. As woebegone a creature as I had ever seen.

It was Phoz.

We shared a hooch.

"What the hell you doing down there?"

"Ditch. They've got me digging a mother fucking ditch."

"They don't have enough ditches around here?"

"Too fucking many, if you want to know the truth. It's for drainage. Carry the water away."

"Why they need to do that? Camp'll dry up without it."

"Mosquitoes. Carries the mosquitoes away, too. Washes them over to Charlie. Gives him malaria. Then we cut off his quinine and he's up shit's creek."

"How much longer you plan to be in that ditch?"

"Till somebody comes along and tells me I can get out."

"Phoz. You can get out."

"I was hoping for somebody with some authority, but who can see with his eyes full of mud?"

"Let's get cleaned up and head over to the club."

"Fuckin-A."

The club had a magic portal. You walked through, you were a civilian. You hoisted a Bud, and you were in your tavern back home.

Didn't make any difference you wore army gear. You wore jeans and a Stetson back home. You weren't a cowboy. Everybody knew you weren't really army, either. The only time you'd ever be would come after you'd been discharged. Then you'd hoist a few in civilian clothes and rap a little about the Nam.

Phoz got to reminiscing about a lady he knew in Wisconsin and their last few days together, when every color he'd seen had been a brighter color than brown. The first warm day of the year. They climbed a hill up on her daddy's farm and laid down under a patch of wildflowers.

> Think about a good time
> Had a long time ago;
> Think about forgetting about your
>   worries and your woes.
> Walking in the sunshine
> Sing a little sunshine song.

When he woke, her pretty lace dress and her slip were bundled up in back of her head. She hadn't worn anything else. Flowers were growing between her legs.

"Now, Phoz. I can't wait anymore. Next week, you'll be in Nam. You may already be dead."

He couldn't believe how beautiful she was. It still made his eyes mist. He brushed the flowers out of the way, and they both gave up waiting. They spent the next three days tangled together in the grass.

It wasn't until he'd gotten out of the ditch that day and picked up his mail that he realized what she meant when she said she couldn't wait anymore.

Besides, she was against the war.

"Ain't no big thing. Plenty of ladies in Wisconsin. But I expect it'll be a while before I forget those flowers."

> Walkin' in the sunshine
> Sing a little sunshine song.
> Put a smile upon your face as if
> there's nothing wrong.

I hoisted a few more than the average. Phoz hoisted a few more than me. After a while we judged it was time to go back to the hooch. Before the shooting started. It's good to remember who you're drinking with, and we were drinking with a lot of angry and armed men, all of whom were getting more beer than they'd ever be allowed anywhere else. Nobody wants to drink in a crossfire.

It was still raining. I followed the boardwalk on the grounds I'd get to the hooch quicker and stay drier. Phoz took the road on the grounds it didn't cross any mud and he seemed likely to arrive cleaner.

I toweled off and lay on my bunk with a blurry copy of *Time*. Phoz didn't show. The trip by road wasn't that much longer. I imagined he'd probably gotten turned around and wound up back at the club. He'd had a hard day.

I was reading "Cinema," reading about *Rachel, Rachel*. One of the movies I'd never see. Part of the culture I'd have to make up on late night TV. Then I heard loud voices in the street and somebody running through the rain and the dark toward my hooch. I had my hand on my rifle for luck when the door kicked open to a rough-looking pair of corporals.

"We found him in a ditch."

"We think it's Phoz.

"Can you identify him?"

There was a kind of squishy shuffling noise and then a shade tripped into the room. "It's him all right." I recognized the uniform.

"What happened?"

"Canal. Mother fucking canal. Walked right into it."

"The ditch you dug today?"

"Fucking-A. Came back the same way last night. Wasn't there then. Just walking along, thinking about this gook chick I know at the laundry. Good thing these corporals here . . . "

> La la la la la dee oh
> Whether the weather be rain or snow.
> Pretending can make it real;
> A snowy pasture,
> A green and grassy field.

■ PX

Cu Chi had a PX. A long, soaking trudge from my hooch, but it was there. A fine big department store filled with Japanese electronics, German optics, Taiwanese clothing, British liquor, and Italian shoes. It could have been a Sears, it was so American. A trip there was a trip home. You could walk the aisles for hours, ogling televisions, radios, serious black 35mm cameras, bug repellent, books, magazines, lamps, chairs, fountain pens, stationery, and zippers. You could buy medals you had never been awarded.

Back of a special counter, colorful bottles stood in glittering extravagance. Cutty Sark and Bacardi, Old Mr. Boston, Beefeaters, and Jack Daniels.

Enlisted men didn't drink liquor, but the army sure let us buy it. It made us feel like grown-ups.

And a soda fountain. A place so American it seemed like it was out of the war entirely. When you went there, you went home. You could sit all afternoon, drinking Coke and eating ice cream where no rocket would find you. Lingering after high school on the other side of the world. A place only Americans could go.

Better than R and R. That only took you out of the war for a while. It didn't make you safe. The tension followed you. Trying to pick up a girl in Sydney or choosing a lady by number in a Bangkok viewing salon. You couldn't relax. But sipping a malted, you were all the way home. You were safe. The war wouldn't start again until you walked out the door. And when things got too hot outside, you could always step back through. To America.

■ THE WELL AT THE WORLD'S END

THE WATCHES OF THE NIGHT

Sitting in bunker 27, rain sheeting down past the gun slit. Waiting to sleep on the shelf, sleep in the hammock, sleep propped against the scope.

The guy on the shelf was there, and so was Nikiyama. He was short and a kind of a golden color. Hawaiian and utterly good-looking. The only enlisted man in Vietnam who wore his uniform like it fit. And took the trouble to clean his boots.

Raymond must have had the night off.

It was at least an hour until dark when I slipped out toward number twenty-six, kicking through clumps of wet grass, looking for privacy.

I found it, a place that was blind to both bunkers. Nobody could see there. I was as invisible as Charlie in the weeds.

I've always liked to piss against a target and, in the middle of that wet field I found one. A waist-high bush, flapping like a marker in the rain. Right in front of a hole, maybe a meter in diameter. Like someone had buried an open garbage can.

I shook off the last drops and walked around to see. The hole looked to be a few feet deep, with small shelves cut into the sides. Then it snapped into focus. Steps. A great round chimney bored at least ten meters into the earth. A double row of rungs cut into the clay and reinforced with wood planks. A neat job, cut as squarely as if it had been dug by a mechanized auger. At the very bottom a secondary tunnel dumped into the shaft.

Straight from the friendly village.

> Like a tunnel that you follow
> To a tunnel of its own,
> Down a hollow to a cavern
> Where the sun has never shown.

Here was an invasion route for all the black-clad killers in two Vietnams to come crawling through, numberless as ants beneath our feet.

Our twisted wire, our rifles, our grenades and our mines, our

artillery and our air support embraced us with their protection.
Blanket on blanket of security. Cu Chi was about the safest place to
be an American you could be. And all those rings of defenses could
do nothing to stop the mindless waves that would someday come
crawling out of that tunnel. The day that happened, the Chinooks
behind us would be scratched from the equipment roster and we'd
all be so many entries in the morning report.

I stared into the pit for all the rest of that long tropical day.

When I pulled back, the clouds hadn't darkened. Nikiyama and
the guy on the shelf were still talking, so it couldn't have been so
long. Still, that tunnel hangs in my memory like a childhood fear.

Nikiyama heard me coming. "Whoa. You don't get any purple
hearts for sprained ankles. See the tunnel?"

"That son of a bitch goes straight toward that friendly fucking
village where they shot Old Joseph from Chitown out of. And Ray-
mond's buddy . . . "

"Sawyer."

". . . yeah, Sawyer. You know how many Charlies could get
through there if they had a . . . "

"One every ten seconds, maybe. Five or six a minute. Maybe
more. Careful you don't drip on the ordnance."

"Those bastards would be all over us. We'd never know they
were here until we heard them, and those sons of bitches don't
make any noise. . . . "

". . . two, maybe three hundred an hour . . . "

". . . move like smoke. We'd be celebrating Tet right here at the
Twenty-fifth."

". . . been checked out. Had a team in here when we first found
it. Climbed to the bottom. It's OK."

"How can a tunnel be OK? Why didn't they blow it?"

"Just didn't. And I can tell you I wasn't gonna. Never know who
you might meet in a tunnel."

While we spoke, a dark figure was walking up behind us.

"Something else. Don't go hanging your head over any holes.
You go sticking it out like a big lollipop and there might be some-
body down there wanting to take a lick off it."

"Sergeant of the guard."

A dark green figure poked its head in the door.

He gave us our instructions: what friendlies were outside the
wire and where they were. When to check in. Two men awake at all
times.

"Anything unusual, let us know."

"Why, yes, Sarge. A tunnel. Just the other side of that flappy bush."

"No tunnels over there."

"I saw it, Sarge. Just now. I got a good look. It's a tunnel."

"It's a well, Troop. Been checked out. It's a well."

"It's got steps, Sarge, and a secondary tunnel heading off toward that friendly village over there. It couldn't . . . "

"Well. It's been checked. It's a well."

"So who dug the son of a bitch? We've been here for years. We don't use wells, not on the blind side of . . . "

"It's a well."

". . . locals didn't come out here and dig it. Who dug it?"

"Maybe it was already there."

"No water. Just rain. And hard clay all the way down."

"Listen, GOD DAMN IT. It's a well. A FUCKING WELL. If that fucking BOTHERS you, climb the FUCK down inside and check it the FUCK out."

I'd run out of arguments by the time he left.

"So what do you think, Nick? You've seen that thing."

"Yeah. I pissed down it. Like you did. Must stink down there."

"You think it's a well?"

"I never saw a well with steps. But what do I know about wells? I tell you, if the army wants a well there, they can have one. I'll leave it alone."

■ TUNNEL RAT

Me? Shee-it no. But Mayguez, he used to go down regular. Puerto Rican. Wiry little guy. Curly hair. Tan like me. The kind the ladies like to get next to, if you know what I mean. He was a tunnel rat. He had the guts to do it, and he was small enough to fit.

"And he'd always been sure he wasn't going to die in a tunnel.

"Platoon couldn't pass a tunnel but we had to check it out. It was always Pancho in there. Had a buddy, a guy from Arizona, part Pima, would follow him anywhere. But Pancho always went first.

"Problem was, some of those tunnels was populated. Mostly the residents would hear them coming and just diddy-mao the area. Mostly. Sometimes they'd back into side tunnels and count on Pancho missing them. And if he didn't, they got the first shot.

"One morning, Pancho and the Indian got into a tunnel that was just the entrance to a whole underground building. They combed through it, but it was abandoned. Not much laying around to liberate, so we called up a chopper load of TNT, and those two spent most of the afternoon placing it in a big pile right in the middle of that hive. Going to bring the house down. They set a fifteen-minute fuse and climbed back to daylight.

"We waited forty-five minutes.

"An hour.

"Nothing.

"Finally, Pancho and the Indian went back to see what had happened. With Pancho in the lead and the Indian right behind, they wriggled down tunnels too small for a grown-up American to get through.

"You couldn't tell nothing from the top. So we just waited. I was playing split with Vegas Bill's bayonet when there commenced a loud bustling sound, gasping and stumbling. Pancho spat out of the ground like a miscued billiard ball. He came down very excited, crossing himself and reaffirming his religious beliefs.

"The Indian came out after a while, too, spitting dirt. No idea what had happened. He'd just followed Pancho down that tunnel. Too low to raise their heads or even see where they were going until they came to the place where they'd left that big pile of TNT.   95

And it was gone. Nothing but packed dirt. A thousand pounds of explosives set to go off, and somebody had stolen it.

"Pancho got curious and led the Indian along a side shaft even tighter than the one they'd come down. They were wriggling along like seals when somebody, crawling up the other way, suddenly clawed and gouged over top of the Indian. He was pinned in the loose dirt. It was too tight to breathe, and he didn't have any idea who was on him. But he just knew he'd been captured. Had a side-arm but he couldn't get at it. Didn't want to shoot down there anyway. Not much air.

"All he wanted to do was get out of there. But he couldn't move. He waited, choking, his face jammed into the dirt, until whoever was on top scrambled on past, kicking him in the head and the back and the calves and bringing down little explosions of dirt every time his heels hit the top of the tunnel. When he finally got by, the Indian was almost too buried to move. But he could, and he crabbed back out, trailing streamers of loose dirt and yelling for Mayguez to follow. When he finally got to the top he weighed as much as one of us, what with dirt in his boots and dirt down his pants and his shirt. His mouth was ringed with a brown crust and he had so much dirt up his nose he was sneezing gravel for weeks. And his eyes were full of dirt and things didn't look any brighter than they had in the tunnel. And there was Pancho. Out ahead of him somehow, kneeling and crossing himself.

"The captain had a little Jack Daniels and brought Pancho around.

"When he went looking for that TNT, it never occurred to him that the thieves might still be nearby. He wriggled along the shaft, his arms pinned to his side like he was a mummy ready for a funeral. He came to a junction, and the only thing he could do was poke his head out and look around. He hadn't seen much when a gun muzzle jammed into his temple. He was as stuck as a cat in a sack.

"He waited a lifetime.

"Waited until somebody pulled the trigger.

"The gun clicked.

"A misfire.

"Pancho's personal time caught up with real time. He scrabbled back out of that tunnel before whoever held that gun could pull the trigger again. He wasn't counting on two misfires in one day.

"The Indian could never figure how Pancho got past him. Or turned around in that narrow tunnel. But he did. I saw Pancho come out first myself. And I saw what the Indian looked like when he came out.

"After that, Pancho was still sure he wasn't going to die in a tunnel. But by then we all knew he was right. He never went back into one.

"And the Indian, he just followed right on behind Pancho."

■ SHARING THE LIGHT

THE WATCHES OF THE NIGHT

". . . you got the times. Check in.

"No friendlies out front. You see anything, report it. ASAP. No firing without somebody says so.

"Bick?

"Two men up at all the times. I'll check back through here later on."

The sergeant of the guard headed off toward number twenty-eight, and we slid up onto the bunker, avoiding the brown spot. Perce was from Gary.

The rain had steamed to a halt. We'd waited all day for the weather to cool down. As it got darker, Perce would talk, and a light would flash over us from across the wire. And I'd nod. Relaxing evening but for the stiff neck from the tunnel in back of my shoulders.

"Hey, Perce, you ever seen that tunnel back there?"

"Shee-it, yeah. Dropped a grenade down there once. Willy Peter. Didn't reckon no frags would do much, but that phosphorous shit don't play. Burned the air right out of the mofo. Smothered all them Congs. Ain't never been none of them mofos come out of there since."

"You ever go down to check?"

"Ain't never been down one of them mofos, but I slept on one once.

"Two-week patrol up to mofo Parrot's Beak. Big nest of Congs over there. We was gonna kick us some ass.

"Second, third night out, we camped up side this stream on a mofo grassy hill, backs to some cliffs. A neat place, like . . . "

A light flashed onto the bunker, washed over us and moved on.

". . . rich folks' yards. Next morning we was out looking for Congs. Couldn't find us none, but a week later we ran into a mess of them the other side of the border. Couple dudes got medevaced back to the world. Left the Congs where their buddies could find
98   them."

"Cambodia?"

"Gots to. That's where the mofo trail come out. How you gonna plug up no trail without you can't . . . "

The light slipped by.

". . . go over to it? We headed back same way we came and liked to walk into a mofo air strike. B-52s bringin smoke no more'n a klick up the road. Those mofos be shakin windows back to Cu Chi. You oughta hear them when they's fallin all around your head. We thought we's bein bombed.

"When it let up, there was craters right in the mofo trail. Hills of dirt and clods all over the place. Big trees lookin like busted pool cues.

"Nobody wanted no truck with no five-hundred-pound duds, so we guided around the area. So tore up nobody recognized it at first. But Sergeant Crocket figured it out from his map. It was that grassy place we camped . . . "

The light pinned us to the bunker and swept on.

". . . on the way out. I was mofo glad we hadn't been campin there that day. Then couple dudes found wofo they been doin the bombin.

" 'Holy shit. Look at THIS bullshit.'

" 'MOFO.'

"Them mofos done blowed the roof off a underground city the size of Fort Bennin. It was like a mofo ant hive. SHEE-IT. If I'd knowed about all what was down there, I'd a enlisted with the mofo Congs.

"Command center. Communications equipment. Ammo dump what the bombs missed. Mess hall. Barracks. Hospital. Nobody to use them now but corpses. They was all still steamin. And some of them was Chinese. Tall mofos in funny uniforms. Six foot, six foot two. Ain't nobody like that growed in the Nam.

"Even had mofo yardmen down there to keep the grassy mound looking natural. She . . . "

The light dazzle-FLASHED—and moved on.

". . . fooled us. Double Dan'd tell you won't the same place, but it was. One of them bombs dug up a busted bayonet I buried so's I wouldn't have to keep totin' it around. That sure was the place.

"We'd camped right on top of that mofo. Had our perimeter out all around the hill. Guards. Claymores. Trip wires. Set out all our shit. And them dudes was under us. And inside us. They probably had doors in the dirt like those hairy spiders on TV. Could have cut us all up. Them mofos bad, bro. They don't play.

"MOFO.

"Never made no noise. Turned their mofo radios down and tip-toed around so's we could all sleep. Next time I'm carryin me a mofo stethoscope. Gonna listen to the mofo. . . .

Flicker . . . FLASH

"Say, bro. That mofo be sayin they ain't no friendlies nowhere tonight?"

We were off that bunker like it was covered with roaches.

He was the first to the phone, and he filed the report. The guy on the shelf was already straining at the pale green landscape inside the scope.

"Damned if I can tell what it is. Every time the light's on us it washes out the scope. Then it moves and the scope settles down and I can't see nothing. . . .

FLASH . . . DAZZLE

". . . but the fucking light sticking over top of the mother fucking rise over there. Ain't never going to figure it out from here. Should inquire of it with some artillery. Leave some evidence to check out in the morning."

I was thinking more in terms of an air strike. B-52s, if it could be arranged. But artillery would at least distract whoever was out there.

The light was in our faces again when a captain and a major stepped down into the bunker. They must have taken the light seriously. It was easier to call in an air strike than get officers out on the line after dark.

The major took the scope. The shapes in it hadn't changed.

"Can you see what it is?"

"Just the light, Major. Can't go look in back of that rise until morning."

"Be gone by morning."

"Artillery. Artillery'd leave some clues. Drop some of them eggs over there. Tomorrow somebody can go out. See what's left."

"Not yet. Don't know what it is."

"Sure ain't nothin of ours. How we gonna find out what it is unless we got something to look at?"

"Not yet. I'm gonna study that thing until it starts shooting or I know what it is."

All the progress those two were making, they'd spend the night with us. And with them around, we really would have to stay awake two by two.

I had work to do the next day.

The three of us sat crowded on the shelf, kicking sandbags and watching the officers look through the scope. Things wouldn't have been more tedious if we had been looking through it ourselves. We were in a Turkish prison. I didn't know how to get out.

But Perce did.

"Uh, Major. You and the captain be using the mofo scope and sitting at the slit and all, does you mind if I goes outside for a while. . . ?"

"And me . . . ?"

"And me, too?"

"I won't be leavin the area. . . ."

"Not us. We'll be right up top. You want us, you just holler, sir."

"Go on up. We'll get you when we leave."

We were out of that bunker like beetles out of a disturbed corpse.

"Jee-zus, Perce. Why didn't you say that about eighteen hours ago?"

"Wanted you dudes preciate it. You glad to be out, ain't you? You know I'm good."

"Ok, good. Why don't you see about getting us some beer?"

"Gots some bitches bringing it over now."

The officers never came up for us. They spent the night pulling our watches, two by two. Or maybe they just slept the way we did. We stayed outside. Sleeping under the clean tropical sky.

I never found out what we saw. Neither did anybody else. I bumped into that major once, down by Phu Cuong village. He'd sent out a patrol the next day, but they hadn't found much. Just tread marks.

■ BLOWING AMMO DUMP

They never tell you how beautiful war can be.

At 14:30 I had gotten as far as the dagger on a motto I was stenciling on a dump truck. I put down my brush and was looking over the cab when the explosion came. Several months' accumulation of captured ordnance went up in a place four or five klicks outside the wire.

Nothing but rice and fields lay between camp and that ammo dump. I saw the whole gaudy eruption. A sudden pink smoke ball maybe one hundred meters across rose stately into the air while shock waves rushed through the grass and the rice toward us. It didn't hit with a sharp concussion but brought a sort of out-of-focus rumble of thousands of shells and rounds and charges and mines all going up at approximately the same time. Having arrived, the rumble rolled around and around as more and more explosives blew.

The cloud drifted higher through the still air, lit from below by colored lightnings from ever more explosions, roiling dust and smoke into the sky. Bright patches, colored by smoke grenades and laced by random cottony trails from escaping rockets, gave the cloud the carnival look of a gaily expanding hot air balloon.

It went on and on like that, the truck shaking as if it were in motion. The cloud kept rising while explosions danced along the ground in endless revue. A circus of ordnance blowing up before my eyes.

If the enemy had captured that ordnance, he would have used it to kill Americans. We blew it up just to keep him from taking it back. We could afford new stuff.

That must have been the best-supplied war in history. Not only for the enemy, with the mountains of material captured from us and the endless river of killing tools rolling down from Hanoi, but for us as well. All a general had to do was requisition something, and a patriotic nation would give him more of it than he should ever have had.

Frugal as the enemy seemed, sorting through all those captured rockets and mines and artillery shells for something he could use against us, I like what we did with them better. We turned them into fireworks. Less wasteful than killing people.

The army could have sold tickets to that show. As it was, they
announced the time and the place. Like for a movie. The only thing
they didn't do was print reviews so we could know whether we
wanted to watch.

All over Cu Chi, come 14:30, men were standing on roofs, and
fifty-five-gallon drums, and in the beds of dump trucks, staring off
to the south, waiting for the torch to be put to a pile of explosives
stacked half as high as the great pyramid.

But for all that beauty rising softly into the afternoon sky, some
portion—maybe half, maybe much less, but some huge number of
shells and rockets and mines—did not explode. It just tumbled into
the air and fell back to the ground in an invisible circle hundreds of
meters around. Ugly burned touchy things, snuggled under the
roots of weeds or sitting quietly in the shadows of rocks, waiting to
remind a generation of passersby of the beauty we saw that day.

■ BOMBING REPORTED ON TV

THE WATCHES OF THE NIGHT

". . . AND NOW, DIRECT FROM THE WORLD, THE ARMED FORCES RADIO AND TELEVISION NETWORK PRESENTS: *ROWAN AND MARTIN'S LAUGH-IN. . . .*"

People wandered in and out, past a couple of privates with eyes like cigarette burns. Derelicts on their third tour.

". . . LITTLE ORPHAN ANNIE, CALL THE EYE BANK. . . . "

They'd arrived as PFCs so long before that it wasn't even the same war. In the order of things they should have been staff sergeants. They'd seen the big buildup when America came to win. By '68 the excitement was gone. We didn't know about winning any more. We were only there to wait out our year. For them it was just too late to go anywhere else.

". . . IT ISN'T THAT I WANTED TO WORK FOR THE C.I.A., IT'S JUST THAT I STILL HAVE FAMILY IN WASHINGTON. . . . "

Phoz knew what burned out those eyes. I guess he figured their ears were shot too, because he told me, right there.

"First day here they looked out the gate and volunteered for permanent KP. Re-upped for the supply room.

"Garrison duty's a drag. Nothing to do but dope."

". . . SOCK IT TO ME. . . . "

The floor rolled, and the hooch shook.

        . . . RUMBLE   RUMBLE   RUMBLE

104   like we had come down range on an artillery barrage.

The television danced across the table. The footsteps of God stalking the corridors of Eden.

RUMBLE   RUMBLE   RUMBLE

". . . HERE COME DE JUDGE
". . . HERE COME DE JUDGE . . . "

I didn't know any place to run, and nobody else seemed to care. When it was over, nothing was hurt, and Phoz was still explaining.
". . . powerful righteous stuff . . . "
"What was that?"
"The rumble? Haven't heard.
". . . don't take much to burn a hole right through your brain . . . . "

". . . FOREST FIRES PREVENT BEARS . . . "

". . . been doing it every night for three years. Don't see nothing but mirages now. Spend their nights dodging shadows and their days bumping into things."

". . . DON'T ADJUST YOUR SET, I'M COLORED . . . "

"Army's glad to have them. Can't do any damage in the supply room. Freed up a couple of clerks for the field. Got no energy. . . . "

". . . IF JAN STERLING HAD MARRIED PHIL SILVERS, DI-VORCED HIM AND MARRIED ROBERT SERVICE, SHE'D BE JAN STERLING SILVERS SERVICE. . . . "

". . . to leave.
"Should have gone to the field. Keeps you clean. Guy burns his brain away out there, he's as likely to shoot you as Charlie. Or just start shooting butterflies. Attracts attention."

". . . WHAT YOU JUST FELT WAS A B-52 RAID ON DU-GIAO, ABOUT 17 MILES NORTH OF CU CHI. NOW BACK TO OUR REGULARLY SCHEDULED . . . "

[Holy Shit, can you feel it *that* far . . . ?]

". . . YOU BET YOUR SWEET BIPPY . . . "

"They're safe enough, but still, the army should have medevaced them out years ago. I guess they just needed somebody in the supply room."

". . . I COULDN'T GET YOU LIFE, BUT I GOT YOU ALTERNATING CURRENT. . . . "

■ PRISONER

John, Harlan H., USA, 1 Lt., 02, Intelligence.

Harlan was from the North Carolina mountains. Boone's Crossing. A place so small that people in other parts of the county weren't quite clear where it was. He grew up about as free as any American ever does. He worked the land, he trained himself to be a solid shade-tree mechanic, and when he was eighteen he won a partial scholarship to North Carolina State. The rest of his expenses he covered by running a cash register in the cafeteria. He never joined a fraternity. He stopped doing what those boys did when he was in high school. He didn't need other people to feel comfortable. Besides, no fraternity ever asked him.

In the spring of 1966, four years and nine months after he went to State, he graduated with a degree in civil engineering and nowhere to go. The only places he knew were Boone's Crossing and the school cafeteria. Neither one was hiring civil engineers.

Back home he looked up his mother's sister, Rebecca, who sat on the draft board when it met over in Asheville. Aunt Becky told him that she drafted people out of those mountains but not right away. She waited maybe a year and a half, maybe more. It was a source of pride. They never had to draft much. People enlisted. Her district had about the highest enlistment rate in the country. Young men glad to serve. Month after month those enlistments came close to filling the quotas. Some months they did fill them.

"I tell you, Harlan, you're a fool to wait for the draft. You reckon on working your daddy's farm until I write you? Waste two years waiting. You could be in and out in that time. Now, you volunteer for the draft, and you got some choice. Not just a rifleman in the rice, thank you kindly."

Harlan drove over to Asheville and signed up the next day. He parlayed his college degree into orders for OCS and a ticket to Fort Benning. Even after five years at State, Harlan was tougher and better with a rifle than any of his drill sergeants. During his second week in Basic they gave him clip-on sergeant's stripes, made him trainee sergeant, and told him that he was responsible for the other men in his platoon. The men respected his quiet toughness, and

107

Cu
Chi

after that, his platoon had the highest rating in its battalion and won an extra three-day pass by way of unit citation.

After OCS, John was sent to the Defense Language Institute in Monterey and spent a year studying Vietnamese eight hours a day. When he was done, there wasn't a person in Vietnam who could talk to him on the phone and not think he was one of them.

In Vietnam, he was assigned to the Twenty-fifth Infantry's Intelligence Section and worked in a compound inside Cu Chi Base Camp. Cu Chi was separated from the outside world by concertina wire and explosives and bunkers. The Intelligence Section was set off inside Cu Chi behind twelve-foot chain link fences strung with barbed wire. Inside those fences, a large dusty barren space surrounded a cluster of low buildings. Nobody outside knew what went on in those buildings. Harlan John wasn't on the outside. He worked in one.

The prisoners came in boxes like everything else in Vietnam, packed away in conexes (containerized exchanges), overseas cargo containers. Scores of conexes arrived from home every day, bringing everything from beer to bullets. There wasn't much to send back to the States, so the containers tended to pile up. They were good for keeping things that needed to be stored. Like prisoners. They weren't made to be broken out of barehanded, and a prisoner put inside would still be inside when you came back for him. At eight feet by twenty feet, those containers wouldn't fit indoors, so they stayed outside, heating in the tropical sun. After a few days in a conex, most prisoners were glad to step out and talk.

Nobody in Intelligence ever saw the prisoners put in the conexes. But every morning they were there, and some enlisted man would bring a stack of files with a brief note on who was in which container—name, where captured, which unit, party rank, and so forth. When the interrogators chose a file, the guards would go to the container, and there the man would be, like a new shipment of some questionable substance, just arrived from home.

John's first prisoner was an anonymous VC captured with a satchel charge outside Long-Thanh. The guards manacled him to a straight-backed chair. Then they waited out back until it was time to take him away.

John set out after that Charlie with all the skills he had practiced but never used.

"What is your name?"

No answer.

Never an answer.

John talked and cajoled and threatened. The prisoner never moved. He might not have understood a word, for all he answered. John kept probing. Jab. Pull back. Jab. Looking for the key to get the man to talk. Never a response. John kept thinking that, if he just knew how to ask the right questions, if he only knew what to say, the man would open up.

> If we could Talk To The Animals,
> Just imagine it,
> Chatting to a chimp in Chimpanzee . . .

"WHY DID YOU HAVE THAT SATCHEL CHARGE?"
No answer.
"WHAT WAS IT FOR?"
No answer.
Never an answer. John had spent a year of eight-hour days learning an alien tongue to come here and talk to terrorists who wouldn't speak. The Defense Language Institute had taught John the language but nothing about the prisoners who spoke it. He needed a course on Oriental murderers.

> If we could talk to the animals,
> Learn their languages,
> Maybe take an animal degree . . .

Finally, John gave up. He was sweating as if he'd spent the afternoon in a conex, and he didn't even know the prisoner's name. The prisoner had won. John called the guards to take him back to his container. John retreated to another room where the major in charge of his section was waiting.

"How'd it go, Son?"

"Nothing. Not a single damn thing. If the rest of the Cong are like this guy, we're wasting our time here."

"They're not. Not all of them. A lot are glad to be here. Just conscripts. They don't want this war. This guy may be something bigger or just a dedicated fanatic. Whatever he is, he knows something we want to find out. He knows who sent him off toward Saigon with that satchel. And who he was supposed to kill."

"Well, I sure can't find that out. I've done everything I know."

"You just weren't trained right. Come on, we'll go talk to our Mr. Charlie together."

The guards had gone through this before and had already prepared the prisoner for the next round. His pants were piled around his ankles and his balls hung down between his legs. A heavy wire, clamped to his scrotum with a painful-looking alligator clip, ran to a switch on the interrogator's desk. Another wire hung waiting. The prisoner's left eye was puffed from a new blow.

John prayed the wires were meant to scare him. While he watched, one of the guards clamped the other alligator clip to the prisoner's foreskin.

"Now, tell him we own his body and we're gonna burn it off piece by piece until he tells us what we want to know. And if he don't tell us damn quick, we're gonna keep burning anyway.

"Tell him we're gonna burn his nuts off first, to show him how it works, and then we're gonna run the juice up and down to give him a feel for the range.

"Tell him when we're done he's gonna have to squat down to piss, just like his whore sister."

A guard flipped the switch and the prisoner howled like a dog. And howled. And wept. And shitted in his chair. And pissed down his leg while the electrodes sparked and crackled in the salt water.

While all John could think about was what his hand-to-hand combat instructor had told his class in Basic: "You must become your enemy. You must get into his skin and think the way he thinks and feel the way he feels. You must see with his eyes and know with his mind."

He knew we would prevail over this prisoner. The man was a terrorist. A murderer. He would have done the same to John if he had had the chance. He would have done it as a matter of course. He would have done it without conscience, and he expected John to do it to him now.

John became one with his enemy. But he knew that being at one with such an enemy was a price he was not willing to pay.

If we could walk with the animals, talk with the animals,
Grunt and squeak and squawk with the animals,
And they could squeak and squawk and speak and talk to us.

When the guards finally turned the electricity off, the prisoner mewled betrayal of his comrades through gobs of puke. But John wasn't there to listen. The major spoke animal, and he could get the information. John just spoke Vietnamese.

There was no place for John in Interrogation after that. He refused his next prisoner and the next. Until the major understood he really meant it. It happened sometimes. John got reassigned, probably wasting a year of expensive government training but surely saving his soul. In the end he knew the major had been right. That prisoner's confession had saved a score of Catholics from becoming martyrs the following Sunday. The thing was, Harlan did not care.

■ MEETING AT NIGHT

THE WATCHES OF THE NIGHT

The moon wasn't up, and we walked with our hands out front. We didn't talk much. Just sat, listening to the dark, one ear over our shoulders. It was a good night for swarming out of a tunnel.

Didn't hear anything at first.

And then we did.

A crushing noise like something very heavy moving our way. Off toward twenty-six.

Something monstrous had got through the tunnel and we were naked before it. Rifles, flak jackets, helmets, grenades—all down in the bunker. They might as well have been at Fort Leonard Wood.

It stopped.

We froze in the darkness.

Waiting.

And then Raymond saw it.

"Over there. Toward twenty-six. In the air, see? Pale. Weird shit."

And then Perce saw it. "MOFO."

But I was the first to make it out and I didn't want any part of it.

A ghostly dagger higher than a man could reach. Along with the motto of the Combat Engineers:

FIRST IN † LAST OUT

I knew that tank barrel. I'd spent the better part of an afternoon painting that motto on it. But it wasn't the time to brag.

"That's some weird shit, man. Somebody'd have to be a real dufous mother to be painting some shit like that on a tank barrel."

"Wofo somebody do somethin like that fo, nohow?"

"Beats shit out of me. Must be some strange kind of dude."

Perce spotted a head poking up out of a hatch and was all over it.

"Wofo you want to paint that trash on your tank fo, nohow? Mofo Engineers ain't no first-in-and-last-out shit. Where was Engineers

in Bolois? Where was Engineers in mofo Pineapple Plantation?
Mofo infantry's first in, last out. Mofo."

He stressed his point with a clot of dirt to a giant gear lying just
back of the tread.

"Cut us some slack, Jack. Some psycho back at the motor pool
painted that shit on there. Every time we check out our tank, there
it is. We got our own bucket of mother fucking green. Paint it out
every night. Paint's gotten so thick, if we ever shoot this thing, we
gotta button up. Chunks'll be flying around like righteous shrapnel."

I eased away, hands in my pockets. Didn't want anybody check-
ing under my nails.

"Don't make no sense to me nohow. Mofo Engineers ain't no
first in, last out shit."

Perce was feeling around for a rock when the barrel swung over
and all he could see was the big eye staring right at him. Raymond
and I had diddy-maoed the area by then. But didn't anything come
of it. Perce was nothing if not adaptable.

"Any you dudes see my mofo contact lens around here?"

Phoz had a one-armed monkey, no bigger than a beer mug. Its arm had been sheared off in some obscure accident he would never discuss. He kept it clipped to trees so it could play outside. That's where I met it. At the foot of a banana tree while I was walking back from the motor pool. It was doing back flips in the dust while three or four men I didn't know squatted in a semicircle, laughing. Phoz was off to the side.

"Lighten up on the little dude. He's no kitten."

"What the fuck, Phoz. I've had guinea pigs bigger than that. Damn thing can't even reach my knee. Can't climb straight, neither."

"Just be careful he don't climb your ass. You bick?"

He didn't bick very well, as it turned out. He would poke the monkey with the toe of his boot and the monkey would flip over backward. Then he would poke it again and the monkey would flip backward again. I couldn't tell when the monkey tired of the game, and neither could he. But the monkey could tell, and when the time came, it swarmed up the boot like ants. And the leg and the shirt and didn't veer off at the shoulder the way monkeys do. It went straight up the face.

Its tormentor never got his guard up. He stumbled backward until the taut chain snatched the monkey from his head, arcing it to the ground with a pair of glasses in its teeth.

The thing was, that guy was right. One-armed monkeys can't climb as well as regular monkeys do. But even with a pair of glasses in its mouth that monkey could climb better than any of us. And that was enough. When it was done, it chittered from the top of the banana tree, turning the glasses over in its feet like it was eating corn.

"MOTHER FUCKER. Get my GOD DAMN glasses out of that GOD DAMN tree."

"He'll drop them when he's tired of them."

"NOW, GOD DAMN IT. Tell him to bring them down now."

"Ain't never listened to me yet. Just be ready to catch."

The monkey was passing the glasses from foot to foot in a negli-

gent sort of way. It was beginning to look like they might be arriv-
ing shortly. But he was only teasing.

gent sort of way. It was beginning to look like they might be arriving shortly. But he was only teasing.

"SON OF A BITCH. I'll shoot that monkey-assed son of a bitch out."

"How you gonna shoot him with your glasses off? You can't even see him up there."

"Full automatic. I sure as shit can spray the son of a bitch out."

Just then the monkey got bored with the glasses. Or maybe it had lost its arm to another glasses owner with a rifle. Anyway, they dropped with a little plop in the dust. The owner dived for them on the ground, sweeping the monkey's chain aside to reach them. That chain had been hanging there all along. He could have jerked the monkey down any time. Phoz figured he just didn't want to.

He went away with his glasses, and the other people drifted after other entertainment and Phoz and I were left with a one-armed monkey chattering overhead. Then it squirreled down the tree and squatted in the dust, looking up at me out of a head like a fuzzy brown tennis ball. You had to admire it, the way it handled that guy with the glasses. He never saw it coming. He knew a hundred ways of stomping a monkey into the dirt, but he never used any of them. Didn't even try to defend himself.

Affectionate little fellow. I began tickling its stomach. In a minute it would roll on its back for a good rub.

"Careful. That other dude wouldn't listen. He's not a kitten."

I knew what Phoz meant. I buttoned my glasses in my pocket and rubbed the monkey again.

A cat thinks a human hand is a mouse, and a dog supposes it is a rag. They'll play with a hand all day, but even a one-armed monkey has hands of its own and knows a hand for what it is: a distraction. The monkey ricocheted off the ground and poked a fist no bigger than a toe into my eye while I thought it was still enjoying itself on the ground. It didn't care that I thought it like to be rubbed.

I should have been wearing my glasses. Never would have gotten the black eye.

■ EVENING

THE WATCHES OF THE NIGHT

The gates to our right closed at 6:00. At about a quarter till, the roads outside filled with dark shapes. APCs moving toward camp. Boxes of Americans home from patrol. We knew them by their color—camouflage. As distinctive as the markings on a mallard.

The enemy had discovered those colors, and those boxes carried the signs of a fight. Dents and burns. Hatches popped open and paint bubbled off. One Charlie with one Czechoslovakian rocket could spatter molten steel from an APC's own armor over a squad of our best men. They wouldn't have been more helpless if they'd been nailed in coffins.

The scars of that fight were left on the bodies of Americans gasping on top. And some, scared past living, had been brought home only as an accommodation to their relatives.

■ NAMING SERGEANT HALYS

One Saturday afternoon I painted my way to a fulcrum point that I didn't notice. All I saw was that I'd run out of paint. And I wasn't allowed to go for more.

"Hey, Halys."

"Huh?"

"Halys. Hey, Halys. I'm out of paint up here."

"What?"

"I said 'I'm out of paint.'"

"WHAT DID YOU CALL ME?"

He slapped his sleeve, jealous of the buck sergeant stripes that it had taken him so long to get. And that he had never earned.

I told you he was touchy about his rank.

"WHAT DID YOU CALL ME?"

If I'd been any other place or it had been any other day, I would have said what he wanted. I would have called him "Sergeant." But it was Saturday afternoon in football season, and I didn't care.

"This is my first name, Troop [slap, slap]. That's what you call me."

And I knew what I was going to call him.

"Hey, BUCK. We're out of paint."

■ SENT TO THE FIELD

There's a reason there are no atheists in foxholes. They're all in church. Religious soldiers get sprung from their foxholes for a few hours on Sunday, so on Sunday, everybody is religious. All the sergeants the army has, with all the plans there might be, can't keep a single PFC from his morning at church.

Cu Chi had a fine-looking little chapel, all white and stained glass, with a pleasant nondenominational chaplain who spoke in a pleasingly modulated voice with the lack of fervor of a South Vietnamese general.

They never let us sleep late, but being in that lazy chapel surrounded by color was the next best thing to going back to bed with the Sunday comics. And while we were there, the work details were passed out at the company. To somebody else.

It was Sunday, the morning after I had insulted Sergeant Halys. I was dreaming of a lazy hour in the chapel when somebody shook my bunk. Corporal Joab.

"Get your ass up. Jeep's leaving as soon as you get your shit together."

"Leaving?"

"Need you down to the bridge."

"Bridge?"

"Guy got himself killed last night. Need an Engineer out there."

"Plenty of Engineers here."

"Halys said you were available."

"Not on Sunday."

"Listen, motherfucker, you be in my jeep when I leave. You bick?"

"Come back after church."

> Oh, you can kiss me on a cool day, a hot day,
>   a wet day, whichever one you choose.
> Or try to kiss me on a gray day, a May day,
>   a pay day, and see if I refuse.
> And if you make it on a bleak day, a freak day,
>   a week day, why you can be my guest.
> But never, never on a Sunday, a Sunday,
>   a Sunday 'Cause that's my day of rest.

"Just get your shit together, God damn you."

It was like a carnival ride, that jeep trip. It was so exciting. It was all blinding air and sudden curves and my helmet shifting around my head as we veered across the highway.

At night the enemy packed our roads with explosives. Antitank mines. Russian mines. Chinese mines. Czechoslovakian mines. A huge gusher of mines rolling down the Ho Chi Minh Trail where we were not permitted to stop them. Corporal Joab was not clear whether the road had been swept yet that morning, so he swerved around any discolorations in his path, guessing them to be the marks of digging. And there were many, as that road was an es-pecial target. It was the MSR—the main supply route—from Cam Ranh Bay.

It had been dug and exploded and repaired until it was as blotched as a dirt track on Sunday morning and Corporal Joab handled his jeep with the enthusiasm of Larry Isley skidding his gold-flecked Dodge into the first turn at Caraway.

He'd glide through the gear box as smooth as if he were pouring motor oil until he was in top gear and keep pressing like an escaped cannonball until he spotted a suspicious patch of road and slam the wheel to one side and down shift. The jeep would spin to the shoul-der, grabbing traction from two wheels and clawing air with the other two. Once we were past the spot, he would oil his way back through the gears to spin around the next dark patch.

Trying to anticipate the next place the jeep would swerve, the spot where I might die, preoccupied me so much that I never got much of a look at the countryside. But I got glimpses. Greens and silvers. Rice and water. Dark palm trees and single-story corru-gated houses set right on the road, like diners back home.

We came on the bridge as suddenly as if it had been a colored spot in the road. It lay around an easy curve and didn't have any more superstructure than the rails on its sides. We couldn't see it from a distance. What we could see was a knot of dusty Viet-namese on both sides of the road. Maybe thirty men and women and children. Squatting around small fires. Eating breakfast from tin pots. Hoboes.

Joab skidded to the left, down a steep bank, and stopped in the shadow of the bridge. I was out as quick as I could throw my gear on the ground and counted myself safer in the land of mine enemy than in that jeep. I never saw it or that corporal again, but I ride with him to this day. Whenever I come to a change in a road, I down

shift around it. That made sense in Vietnam. Now it's just a super-
stition. But it makes me feel young and alert, and I like the feeling.

Another soldier ejected with me. There must have been two
casualties the night before. We watched the jeep circle—back
down the road—blessing the ground beneath our feet.

"What is this place?"

"Beats shit out of me."

So we stood and waited.

Bootsteps in the dust. A lanky black soldier strolled out from
under the bridge.

"Sergeant Stamford, gentlemen. Welcome to Phu Cuong bridge."

■ **PHU CUONG**

■ DAY PATROL

I tossed my gear onto a bunk and squatted around a kettle with half a dozen strangers. Cardboard boxes were scattered over the bare floor.

"Grab a can of C's for the pot, brother. . . . "

He was swarthy with a rough face and a black mustache.

". . . just try not to get turkey. Too much in there already. Been skimming the grease into the fire, but you want to be careful. If it flares up, it'll scorch your hair and make your helmet chafe. . . . "

Where our army went, America went, too. From the opulent underground golf courses beneath Saigon to the slow days of the American rummy there under the bridge, we brought all of America with us.

". . . Jake Gyre. Friends call me 'Short.' Tell you about that sometime. DEROS in a few weeks. They gonna send me home. Requisitioned me a first-class boatman to take my place. But I didn't expect you to get here so quick. . . .

(Boatman?)

"Been at the bridge here about four months, myself. Where you been stationed, you know, just since you got in country?"

I couldn't think of an answer. Jake stared at me until he had it figured out.

"Just out of boat school? That it? Ain't no big thing. Least you know enough you ain't going to get somebody killed."

(Boat school?)

It got quiet again. Then:

"SHEE-IT."

"Sergeant Halys wanted to get me killed."

"Well, what the hell's he got against me? I kind of expected a cherry boy, but I always thought I'd get one who'd been in a fucking boat."

His dark mustache hovered while his sharp black eyes settled on me. At last he was decided.

"Well, I'm going to by God do it. I'm going to teach you my boat. And I'm going to leave it to you when I go. You'll be the best fucking driver on the fucking river. And I'll be back in Pine Bluff watching you on television.

123

"God help you if you let anything happen to my boat."

I felt like Saint Peter had opened the door.

"Got a patrol at 2:00. Go down to the dock. We're the nearest boat to the bank. The manual's in the little hatch on the right."

But it didn't show how to drive the boat. It just showed parts. An exploded picture. Rudder shot off to the rear. Steering wheel and gas tank blown straight up. Lights blasted out to the sides. Cleats and gears, sprockets and sockets, screws and boat hooks and switches, and the gas cap, and glass and steel and rubber spewed in every direction in an expanding cloud of shrapnel. And each part numbered and connected by a straight line to the place on the boat where it had been.

And an entire six-cylinder Chevrolet marine engine had blown out to one side and had burst, in a spectacular secondary explosion, the cylinder heads and pistons and spark plugs and fan belts and radiators, wires, and metal. More rushing death. I enjoyed those pictures. Where else would I get the chance to see an exploded boat?

Four hours pass quickly when your first patrol is at 2:00.

At about a quarter of, the dock was bristling with infantry. Helmets, flak jackets, bayonets, rifles, cameras, tape decks, machine guns. Grenades hanging like apples.

Jake and I waited while they trooped on board.

Then he made each of those tough soldiers put on a life jacket. Motherly. Like putting seat belts on children.

When he had the passengers the way he liked, Jake hit the buttons. The big engines hummed like the diesels in a battleship. He backed away from the dock and shoved the levers forward. We all lurched back. Those boats could manhandle floating pieces of steel. With nothing more than us to carry, they roared downstream like righteous anger.

Until that moment I never thought we could win. Everything I'd learned—even in training—was that the enemy were better soldiers. Tougher, more adaptable. More committed. But when I felt that power churning through my legs, I knew it didn't have to be so.

In that boat we would go to the enemy all along the river and he would not show himself. He would not fight. Night attacks and assassinations and murdered village chiefs would be his way.

But we went where America willed, and we carried America's will wherever we went. And we were proud. A reminder to the enemy—every day he stepped to the water and every night he huddled at home, listening—that the United States was there.

That afternoon the bank was a blur of palm trees and hooches and smiling farmers who waved by day and carried the news of our passage by night. We were in the lead boat. Jake guided off landmarks I could never see. In time he powered back and arced into a stand of flooded trees. A forest drowned where the river had spilled through its embankments. He cut the engines and we drifted quiet in there. No leaves. No undergrowth. A desert of flat water and dead trunks. We could have boated for miles.

The grunts piled into the water. Thigh deep. Nobody could see the bottom. So much equipment they would drown from a leg wound and they had to keep their heads up in case they were ambushed. Like so many buoys.

Safer on the boat. Charlie got one clean shot and that was it. Then the levers would be so far forward, he'd get whiplash trying to follow us around.

"So when do we pick these guys up?"

"Don't. They're walking out."

"God help them."

They slid into the trees in two lines.

It was all so quiet. Nothing but the small splash of their knees. They could have been leaves dropped on the water.

Jake didn't make much noise either. But at the time I thought he'd dropped a chain into the boat. He was pouring swamp water into the water jackets around the motors.

"Not supposed to do this, you know. Supposed to use distilled water. But the manual says when you're out of distilled water, yellow swamp water will do. And both jackets leak."

When the last grunt was over the side, I went to cast off. And the rope swam like fever. And so did the tree it was tied to. Twisting with ants. Ragged lines of ants scrambling up the trunk and back down. Purposeful. A whole nation of ants trying to escape their world down the same paths they had taken before. And before. And before that. Along the same closed circuits they had coursed through all their lives while somewhere back of a piece of broken bark an ant queen churned out more eggs to take up the march when these children faltered.

And then they had found our rope. And swarmed over it.

I pulled it in and slapped it on the hull. And ran it through the water. We didn't want any ants.

Jake roared us out of the trees and up the river, an invitation to any enemy who dared. Even with the infantry gone, none did. We were America's finger in their face.

When we got back, the dock was stuck so high out of the water, I couldn't see over it.

"Hell of a tide they got here. Water runs out. Then it sucks back up stream, faster than you can swim. Dufous river runs backward half the time."

Jake put a couple more cans of yellow water into the motor and we climbed out. It was like scaling a cargo net.

■ W. P. GRENADES

A bright flower of death. I could hardly see it in the glare, it had been so dark under the bridge. Hundreds of petals. Golden tipped. White. Shooting outward like exhaust from skyrockets and then slowing down. And drifting away.

Frank Tubb was there. He drove one of the other boats, but just then he was standing to the side, waiting for the smoke to thin. Sometimes, when it did, I could just see a wire trash basket glowing through the haze. Then Frank would toss in two or three dark objects and scramble back out before the new streamers could burst over him.

Whatever was happening, it was beautiful. Soft shapes glowing pastel in the afternoon sun. Expanding and fading and expanding again. I'd never seen anything like it.

"Willy Peter . . . "

"Willy who?"

"Peter. White phosphorous. Didn't you throw some in Basic?"

"Had KP that day."

"Got a couple of crates here. Out of date. So we can't use it on Charlie. Might not work and Charlie would throw it back. Then it would work for sure.

"Or it might go off in your hand. One of those little gobs'll burn all the way through. No way to scoop it out. Water'll just make it explode. Got to cut it out with a bayonet while it's popping and crackling like fatty bacon and the victim is screaming and crying and fighting. Then it leaves a poisoned hole. Won't ever heal. The rest of your life you can shoot marbles through it.

"Truth is, ain't nothing wrong with these things. Only the date stamp's gotten old. How'd you like to be a Charlie in that trash basket? You'd be too busy dancing around and hollering to throw anything back.

"You think they're somethin up here. You ought to see them in the water. That really sets them off."

He lobbed a couple in the river. They disappeared with little splashes. Those grenades were maybe twenty feet deep when they burst. Phosphorous heaven. A quarter of an acre of water lifted from the river. Heat and gases blasted out. When it was over, 127 small waves slapped across one another and a venomous mist drifted over the water. Better than Yellowstone.

It woke Sergeant Stamford.

"TUBB. What did I tell you about throwing those things into the river? Get over here. NOW."

Frank tossed an armload in the trash basket as he went.

■ SHOWDOWN

"Cherry boys" they called us. New guys. Me and the soldier from South Carolina who had ridden out with me. He didn't seem glad to be there, which was a pity. He didn't have anywhere else to be.

He hung back and was a trial to Frank, who was supposed to train him. Frank cursed and stalked and threatened. Nothing worked. The guy just became more hesitant.

It was a mismatch, Frank and that guy. Frank was so loud and not very analytical about what he said. And with a kid's sloppiness he was the center of a lot of accidents. But you knew if you were in trouble he would be at your side, cursing in his exuberance. He might shoot you out of the confusion of his own energy, but at least he would shoot. The guy from South Carolina might never shoot at all. Afraid of making things worse.

Not much to do at night. No television. No enthusiasm to write home. Just a country music station Frank had come up with. Frank and Hank, and Lefty and Lester, and Skeeter and Tammy and Dotty and Dolly, and Bobby and Bobbie, and Charlie and Charley and Charly, and Ernest and Ernie and Earl and Merle and Pearl. All come to Vietnam.

Frank would hum along, never quite sure whom he was humming with. He would ask Jake. Jake was from Arkansas.

"Hey, Jake, who's that?"

"Who?"

"Roy or Merle?"

"Merle. It's Merle."

"I thought it was Roy."

"Merle."

"Sounds like Roy to me."

Then Frank would come to me for a second opinion.

I didn't know Merle. But Frank was usually wrong, and Jake was right most of the time. So I'd go with Jake.

"Merle."

Jake came to believe I was an expert on country music and Frank, not wanting to be left out, agreed.

Just us and a few others under the bridge. And Jesus Ripole.
Mostly Ripper sat alone. He didn't want the company.

I never found out how long he'd been in Vietnam. But it was too long. He was past being a danger just to the enemy. You could see it in his gaunt face and his hollow gaze. Violence had filled him up.

One night he came in, carrying an M16. Looking for Frank.

"Where is that God damn Frank fucking Tubb? WHERE IS HE, GOD DAMN IT?"

Right there with us, as it turned out. And Ripper had gotten his attention. But they didn't approach. Just yelled across me and Jake and the guy from South Carolina.

"GOD DAMN IT, TUBB. YOU GOT ANYTHING TO SAY BEFORE I BLOW YOUR ASS TO HELL?"

Frank didn't, and Ripper kept yelling.

"You know where I've been, ASSHOLE? I've been tied to that FUCKING LOG BOOM for two MOTHER FUCKING hours. You know why, COCK SUCKER?"

Frank didn't.

"I got a God damn piece of rope caught in my prop, dick brain. A God damn piece of rope that you said wasn't . . . "

"It wasn't. I cut it off this morning."

"Then it fucking grew BACK, asshole, cause it sure tangled in my fucking prop."

"I cut it off, GOD DAMN . . . . "

"You calling me a liar? You do, and I'll tie your cock sucking fat SELF up in that mother FUCKING rope that's not there. . . . "

And a tangle of wet fibers splashed against Frank's ear.

". . . you dufous cock sucker. Tell me again that wasn't there."

"God damn you, Ripper. You're the asshole got himself hung up out there."

"Why, you SON OF A BITCH, I'll . . . "

"WHAT? What did you say?"

"I said that . . . "

"YOU LEAVE MY FAMILY OUT OF THIS OR I'LL KILL YOU. YOU UNDERSTAND ME? KILL YOU."

"What?"

"What you called my mamma. I'll kill you."

"Son of a bitch?"

"I warned you, GOD DAMN IT." Frank had his rifle in his hand. Ripper already had his rifle. The rest of us were outside by then, straining to see whether the weapons were set on full automatic or just single shots. Until Jake walked between them.

"Put them down, assholes. I've got a rifle, too. We all do."

Only he didn't have his with him. He didn't need it, though. They were glad of the opportunity.

■ NVA SAPPERS

Sappers, gentlemen. NVA regulars. A whole company of them. Do nothing but bridges.

"Did a number on a big highway bridge out of Nha Trang back last winter. In and out before we could catch up to them.

"Made their way back north in small groups, us looking for them all the way.

"Then R and R, new equipment, new training. And a new target.

"Could be any of four bridges. Three on the coast. The other's here. At Phu Cuong. We've been waiting to see which route they took south.

"We lost them six days ago. Moved out somewhere. If they're coming down the coast, the Third and First Marines, the Americals, an Arvin airmobile division, and some bored naval gunners will stop them. But if they're on the Trail, it'll be up to us. A platoon of wolfhounds, a company of Arvins, and you boat drivers.

"Found them this morning. Just inside Laos. At the head of the Ho Chi Minh Trail."

"So we got an air strike going after them or what, Sarge?"
"You kidding me, Troop? Laos's a neutral country."

■ HAND GRENADE

H ere's how a grenade works.
   Brittle case. Mild steel to shatter into random gray fragments.
Hard steel spring coiled tightly inside, notched to fly into thousands of bright hot pieces. An evenly expanding cloud of death to all God's creatures within eight feet. And half within twelve feet. And to others beyond that.

■ FEELING AT HOME

THE WATCHES OF THE NIGHT

The bridge lay on eight big concrete piers. The piers were fenced below the water. Chain link to keep out divers. Eighty feet to the bottom. The tallest fences in the world, stuffed with concertina wire. Greaves of crusty chain mail.

And guarded by log booms. Logs like utility poles strung end to end across the river. Upstream and downstream from the bridge, they blocked boat traffic. An enchanted circle of logs. A rosary tossed on the river.

Bunkers crowded beneath the bridge, hanging from the road like wasps' nests or built low in the piers near the water. Upstream bunkers. Downstream bunkers. Right-bank bunkers. Left-bank bunkers. Squat guard towers on the road, a tank on top and a searchlight flicking on the water at night.

And the boats. Every night we went out looking for divers. But we never found any. The river was a stream of opaque mud with dark holes cut from the surface where the shadows fell. Divers didn't have to worry about us.

We tried to find them, though. We cruised around the piers in noisy figure eights, shedding explosives like pennies from a Mardi Gras float. Grenades and TNT bombs. It was like hunting for bottom fish, hoping something would float up.

The people in the bunkers did the same thing. Bombs and grenades.

They had a quota. They dropped and pitched and flipped and flung and bobbed and tossed over their shoulders, and they never looked down. They weren't thinking about boats.

When we were done cruising, we'd tie up to a pier and tell them where we were and hope they remembered.

Wasn't much to do on the water. Just talk. Jake would tell me what it was like to be in Vietnam. What to look for. How to keep alive.

He talked about things I'd never seen. Strange happenings and fantastic people. A distant world in another time. It was like fairy tales.

134

"Once upon a time when I was a cherry boy, there was a place in
Cu Chi where we'd sun ourselves in the afternoon. A long hillside where we could listen to the radio and feel like we were back home . . . "

Plsssh . . .

A grenade in the river . . . three . . . four . . . BWAAAMMM. Not very close.

Five-second fuses.

They always went off underwater. Deep enough to swallow the frags. It may have been deep enough to stop a diver. I never knew.

"There was a mortar behind us. Somebody was always shooting it. We could hear the 'thwoomp' as the shells dropped in the tubes and the rushing sound the air makes as they arc overhead. We'd talk some, then 'thwoomp . . . hssssh.' Never paid them much attention. They were ours.

"It was like being at a ball game. You lay back in the bleachers, catch the sun, and talk. Every now and then you hear something going on, but it's not the reason you came.

plsssh . . .

. . . BWAAAMMMMMMMMMM

"One afternoon a mortar went 'twnnggg' instead of 'thwoomp' and somebody yelled 'short round.' I barely heard him over Chet and Tammy."

plsssh . . .

BWAAAMMMMMMMMMMMMMMM

. . . plsssh . . .

. . . BWAAAMMMMMMMMMM

Those were closer, but I figured Jake knew what he was doing.

"I didn't know from shit about short rounds. And I felt safe there. So I just kept nodding along. I was the only person left on that hillside."

plsssh . . .

. . . BWAAAMMMMMMMMMM

plsssh . . .

PLSSSH . . .

. . . BWAAAMMMMMMMMMM

PLSSSH . . .
. . . BWAAAMMMMMMMMMM
BWAAAAAMMMMMMMMMMMMMMMMMMMMMMMM

Those bastards were falling like rice at a wedding.

"When I finally realized what was going on, I was spraddled in the dirt listening to a dud tumbling . . .

PLSSSH . . .
PLSSSH . . .
BWAAAAAMMMMMMMMMMMMMMMMMMMMMMMM
PLSSSH . . .
BWAAAAAMMMMMMMMMMMMMMMMMMMMMMMM
BWAAAAAMMMMMMMMMMMMMMMMMMMMMMMM

". . . right past my ear. Landed between my legs. On its tail. That's when I first really noticed the mortars.

"You want to live, you pay attention to the background.

"And another thing. Don't go listening to no stories while folks are throwing hand grenades at you, neither."

■ DAYTIME OFFICERS

We hid our rank from Charlie. No brass, no yellow stripes or bright patches. Two hundred years of strutting tradition set aside for dark symbols. The enemy shot at leaders.

But we couldn't hide our people. Officers and noncoms stood out, clipped and starched. Examples to the men. Charlie didn't have to see our rank. He only needed to see us.

Officers weren't out there much anyway. They never rode on our boats, and none were stationed under the bridge with us. They would show up when the sun was high, talk to Sergeant Stamford, and leave with hours of bright sky and well-lit road to spare.

They could run things better from a central base. It just made sense.

> Got a good reason
> For taking the easy way out.
> Got a good reason
> For taking the easy way out now.
> She was a day tripper,
> One way ticket,
> Yeh!

■ MAIL CALL

S ometimes we got mail. When it began to pile up back at Cu
Chi and the clerk could find a jeep headed our way.

It was always more than we deserved. None of us wrote much, even though we had plenty of time. Home was so remote, just abstractions. Girls we hadn't met. Jobs we were going to get.

It was the folks back home who felt the loss, or maybe the sense of duty, that makes people write. Parents wrote, and sisters wrote who had never written anybody. They wrote about the way it was in Atlanta. Letters in the southern manner. Not complaining. Never mentioning disappointments.

Georgia, Georgia, a song of you
Comes as sweet and clear as moonlight through the pines.

But of all of them, none of my draft-age friends ever wrote. They were teaching or in the Peace Corps or in graduate school or becoming fathers. Thinking about other things.

■ INSPECTING DEFENSES

Inspecting the defenses.
   "Take us to the next pier."
   And slowly around it. Water lapping through concertina and chain link.
   "How deep's it get here, soldier?"
   "About eighty feet, sir."
   "Water seems okay up here. What's it like down there?"
   "Muddy, sir."
   "Well, looks fine up here."
   It did look fine up there.

". . . in a speech this afternoon before a group of labor leaders in Pittsburgh."

". . . and now, gentlemen, I give you the next president of the United States of America: HUBERT . . . HORATIO . . . HUMPHREY.

clapclapclapclapclapclapclapclapclapclapclapclapclapclapclap
clap clap   clapclap . . . clap clap . . . clap
. . . clap   clap

". . . you know and I know and the great American people know that Richard Nixon is no different from George Wallace and that they both stand for reaction and recession. . . .

clapclapclapclapclapclapclapclap clapclap clapclap
clap   clap . . . clap . . . clap   clapclap

". . . it is a crime. It is a crime against every one of us if any one of us goes to bed cold or hungry. And that crime is the root of the violence and the disorder in our nation. We can solve crime and disorder, and when I am president we WILL solve it, by attacking the underlying social and economic inequities that cause it . . .

clapclapclapclapclapclapclapclapclapclapclapclapclapclapclap
clapclapclapclapclapclapclapclapclapclapclapclapclapclapclap

clapclapclap clapclap . . . clap . . . clapclap
clap   clapclap

clap

". . . I tell you, a new day is coming. We can and we will increase the benefits for all our retired and elderly citizens on social security so they can have the standard of living they deserve.

Everybody have you heard?
He's gonna buy me a mockingbird . . .

"Bring prosperity to everyone in this nation and jobs for all . . .

> And if that mockingbird won't sing,
> He's gonna buy me a diamond ring . . .

". . . Nixon can never end the war in Vietnam. He's one of the military industrial complex men who have little regard for peace. When I am president I will work to end the war. I'll institute a policy of de-Americanization to bring the boys home. . . . Halt bombing of the North. . . . Cut down on American offensive operations. . . . Phased withdrawal of all foreign troops. . . . Negotiate with the Russians. . . .

> Hear me now and understand
> He's gonna find me some peace of mind.

". . . reappraise our international role. . . . Guard against over-commitment abroad . . . loyal to President Johnson's policies . . . more material assistance to police and courts . . . 50 percent across-the-board increase in social security payments . . . I think that, negotiations or no negotiations, we could start to remove some of the American forces as early as 1969 or late 1968. . . . "

> And that's why I keep shoutin in your ear
> Sayin wo, wo, wo, wo, wo

When I couldn't stand any more, I switched him off, and there was Sergeant Stamford, shiny and black in the tropical sun.

"You know, if it came to it, because of the war issue I'd vote for Wallace before I'd vote for that man."

■ SEXY MACHINERY

Clank. Clank. I'm a tank.

The machinery of war. It was beautiful. Treads and turret and drive wheels and bulging armor and periscopes and hatches. And slender, menacing cannon.

Sexy. It touched you in a place from which you could not answer back.

The younger you were, the harder it touched. War is for children. Vietnam was for nineteen-year-olds. Babies. What did they know?

They joined up from all over America and especially from the South, out of love for their country and for that wonderful equipment. So they could slip through jungles with grenades clipped to their belts and so they could spew burning tracers into the shadows. So they could swing the big gray guns to targets over the horizon and so they could come screaming out of the sun carrying $300,000 worth of rockets and $50,000 worth of bombs to a straw hut.

Our best kids.

The government told them it was patriotism. But what does a nineteen-year-old know?

■ GUARDING THE BRIDGE

A tank squatted on our bridge. A barrier against invasion by river. Its long barrel pointed downstream, toward Saigon and the sea. Toward our own people. One gun to close a river.

But it was more than we needed. There was never much traffic under that bridge, and when the invasion came, it came in little boats drifting in ones and twos down from Cambodia. Nothing for a big gun to shoot.

And nobody much to do the shooting. Just a few Americans trying to puzzle out an invasion they could not see. Knights standing watch against the plague. Rattling lances and waving smoke bombs. Chanting and inventing prayers. Just charms to ward off fear.

We carried rockets, automatic rifles, machine guns, rocket-propelled grenades, and hand grenades. All of it no more than charms against fear. We flashed our swords in wild challenge against the air while the enemy slipped in as easily as fleas through the joints in plate armor.

■ WASHING THE TANK

I hadn't known that tank could move. It just sat on the bridge like a stationary gun mount until, one afternoon a head, looking like an old leather rugby ball, popped out of the driver's hatch. Then two soldiers in green shorts climbed on top and another stepped in front, leading it down to the river. Next to us.

They took helmets and buckets and a white bar of soap and began to throw yellow water over dusty hot metal, thinking they could clean the tank that way. Who could see where the tank was dirtier than the water they threw over it?

When they were finished, when the barrel had been sponged and the periscopes wiped, when the treads and drive wheels had been picked clean and the armor rubbed to a dull green, they left the tank where it was and waded deeper in the river. And went swimming.

The machinery of war. Even Vietnamese kids thought it was beautiful.

When the Americans stumbled back out of the river, hair slick and shorts grabbing their legs, kids were swarming over the tank like ants over a dead beetle. Then there was screaming and the *plat plat* of hard feet on mud.

They got away. All but one. He'd slid down the driver's hatch and when he looked back out, he was surrounded by soldiers.

He was out of there like bees, but he didn't get far. He came barreling around the tread and into a blond gunner carrying a ten-gallon drum. Caught like a rat under a trash can.

But the gunner just dumped the water on him. The kid slid away, cursing.

"Hey. Fuck you, GI."

"Hey, fuck you, too, kid."

A kid could do worse than get caught stealing a tank by a wet American.

When the kids were gone, the gunner climbed up and emptied the drum over the turret. And made a little speech I couldn't hear.

It reminded me of a baptism I once saw when Pastor Derek of the Mount Nebo Gospel Church of Roswell (Pentecostal) baptized a '53 Ford pickup in the Chattahoochee. It didn't do any good, though. The pickup rolled off the bluff on the way out. Seventy feet

back down to the water. The brakes were wet.

I couldn't understand how these men had sinned so that they needed to cleanse their very tank. Anger. Hatred. Cursing God. Despair. Even killing, if it worked out. They could do all those things in the tank. But war in a righteous cause is no sin. And those men were no sinners.

And who could open his spirit to the Song Saigon? A river carrying the corruption of a million souls, so many had washed there. All the sorrows of a wounded land sliding under our bridge, rolling swollen to the sea and then back again on the tide forever. So much sadness and hurt. Could anyone heal in such water?

". . . sick, really sick, to see Americans, American boys and girls who never had to fight for their country, carrying those flags outside the recruiting center! And having to listen to what they said! . . ."

"If they could just spend a day—one single day—with you and the other brave soldiers they would learn something, I can tell you . . ."

". . . so proud you fought in the battle of Saigon and not the battle of Chicago . . ."

Letters from people I'd never met. From people I remembered only as friends my parents talked about.

Letters about politics. What the writers thought we shared.

I never answered those letters. I couldn't think of what to say. Besides, they never seemed to offer correspondence.

■ HA

Ha was Chinese, and that was his sorrow. An ethnic China-man raised among people who had had bad experiences with almost all foreigners but with Chinese in particular.

Being Chinese didn't insulate him from being drafted into the South Vietnamese army, an army whose social positions were based on rank and whose ranks ran from full general down through private among the ethnic Vietnamese, every one of whom out-ranked a Chinaman.

When Ha got assigned to the Arvin unit stationed out at our bridge, no punishment was too tedious, and no job too dirty, to be given to him. For hours every afternoon he would stand in the hot sun, holding his rifle at parade rest, while his comrades loitered in the shade of their bunkers. We could never determine his infrac-tions, and I am not sure he knew what they were either. But we all knew why he was out there in the sun.

The experience didn't seem to make him bitter, though. He kept himself bright eyed and cheerful, the way Orientals teach them-selves to be, but got away when he could. Since he had no place in his own society, he sought out ours. In the end he spent so much time with us that it is he I remember when I think of the Viet-namese. In my memory he honors his countrymen much more than they ever honored him.

■ STEEL WRENCH

Hot afternoon and my back was wet on the bunk. Dreams of Charlie. Black pajamas darting through our area, too close to shoot. Plastic rifles too delicate to swing.

I stretched and gathered myself awake. An Arvin stood at parade rest in the tropical sun, and the big steel wrench still glittered on the sandbag. As big as a weighted bat, none of us knew where it had come from. But when the time came, I was going to be right there with it, swinging.

■ IN THE JEEP WITH TONY

R osicrucians."

"Rosy Whatshuns?"

"Rosicrucians. Got some of their stuff here. Don't send it to just anybody, you know."

He pulled out a pile of mimeographed papers, stapled together.

LEARN THE SECRETS OF THE AGES

Tony Paradise kept weights next to his bunk and spent most of his time pressing and curling. Rangy muscles crowded beneath his skin. Hard. A Viking. Or a street fighter from some northern slum. Hell's kitchen. With long hair he would have looked dangerous. As it was he just seemed a little unbalanced.

He worked at night, driving a jeep. Hauling around a big square spotlight. Trying to illuminate Charlies before they could contract down their holes like startled worms.

Wasn't any point to it, though. He wasn't allowed to shoot.

Tony wasn't very bright, but he wanted to do bright things. So he read sometimes. Offbeat religious stuff. Pamphlets he sent away for. Ads clipped from the Sunday magazine. Embarrassing. We laughed at him.

One night he invited me to sit in his jeep a few hours and wave a searchlight around. I was glad to get out from under the bridge.

The light was mounted on the jeep like a huge crate poised over the cab of a forklift. It was so big he could have hired it out for shopping center openings.

We moved a hundred meters up the road and waited. Tony didn't do anything.

"Not yet. Charlie don't come running out when it first gets dark, you know. Waits for things to slow down. That's when I switch this baby on.

"And sometimes he's there. Some nights they'll all be there, their little eyes staring up like roaches when you turn on the kitchen light.

"Thing is, once I switch on, Charlie knows where we're at. Then I got to move."

149

He chatted, and I listened. Sometimes he'd switch on the light and then drive somewhere else.

Then the radio would rasp static. Tony would answer with the destination.

. . . CROCKLLLttthree to
SPLLLLTTower . . . BZZZzzzB . . . depeCROCKlll . . .

"East bridge tower."

And we would move again.

And in between he would talk about the Rosicrucians.

"You should join."

"What for?"

"Mind control."

"You're into mind . . . ?"

"Well, I'm from New York City, aren't I?"

"Is that where the Rosicrucians are?"

"No. It's where witches come from. Everybody knows that. Just look at *Rosemary's Baby.* Even my own people have the Powers."

Tony moved us downhill.

"Do Rosicrucians run in families?"

"Sure. You take my sister. She's got the Powers. One day she was sitting in the kitchen when she got this feeling our brother had to be checked up on. He's never been quite—well, you know— right, and . . ."

"It does run in families."

". . . she hadn't seen him in a long time. So she went downstairs and there he was, chopping up the goldfish with a spoon. I told you she had the Powers. But she never developed them. That's what I'm doing."

"Over here?"

"They mail me the lessons."

"You're taking a correspondence course in witchcraft?"

"I'm developing my Powers."

"So what do you learn?"

"Oh, you know. Out-of-body stuff. Auras. Divine lights. Talking with the other side. Things like that."

"You can do those things?"

"I'm just on my third lesson."

"Well, what can you do now?"

"Make paper spin around in a milk bottle."

"What?"

"Stick a needle in a cork and put the cork inside a glass milk bottle. Then balance a strip of paper on the needle. Like a little propeller. Got a drawing of one in here. I can make it spin one way. Then stop and go the other way. Just from concentrating on it."

"You did that?"

"Sure."

"Could you do it for me? Make the paper spin?"

"Where can I get a milk bottle in Nam?"

"How long you been over here?"

"Nine months, come the sixth."

"How long you been sending off for those lessons?"

"Three, four months."

"So where'd you get a glass milk . . .?"

SNAPoke yo CRACklesam for wesWHIZZZzzzPop

"By the wire on the west side."

"You ever think about driving a cab when you get back to the world?"

"Hey, who told you that? You got the Powers, too. You should take the course. I'll write the address down."

"I don't want it."

"You can't just throw the Powers back in God's face."

"I don't have any Powers, Tony."

"You believe in the river, don't you? Well, believe in the Powers. Just look at my Aunt Theresa."

"Your what?"

"Mother's sister. She can see the future. Saw Johnson would beat Goldwater. How do you like that?"

"Everybody saw that. It was in all the papers."

"But she knew it. And she knew I'd be drafted."

"We were all drafted, Tony."

"I tell you, she saw it."

"Well, does she tell you about any of those things before they happen?"

"Sometimes. She didn't tell me about being drafted, though. What could I do? But as soon as I opened the letter, she said, 'I knew it. Knew it all along. They're going to send that boy to Vietnam.'"

"But what did she predict BEFORE it happened?"

"Everything. She predicted everything before it happened."

"WHAT THINGS DID SHE TELL YOU ABOUT?"

"The Kennedy assassination. He didn't get elected until the next day, but when he did, she looked up and said, 'The Masons will get him. They'll never stand for him to live,' and she was right."

SP-Lttt top ilPrzzzzpppoun the nePRZRZRZRZZZZZ

"How about you? Can you predict things?"

"Sure. The Rosicrucians taught me."

"Go on and predict something, then."

"Take the course and you can do it yourself. I'll send in one of those little forms for you when we get back."

"I still want you to predict something."

"Doesn't work that way. It's got to come to you. When it does, you know it. Then later it happens. If you took the course, you'd know this stuff."

"So what's come to you so far?"

"Hey, cut me some slack. I just started that section."

"Tell you what. You predict something that happens. And then I'll believe you."

"And you'll take the course?"

"And I'll take the course."

Some promises you know you'll never have to keep. But on the way back, Tony kept confirming that one.

"You mean it. One prediction and you'll take the course? Just one prediction? You really mean it?"

It didn't seem like anything to worry about.

■ CALVIN ROSE

Tony Paradise had a partner. Calvin Rose. They worked together, but Calvin was in charge. He was a sergeant. He'd done better in jeep school.

Calvin lifted weights, too. Right along with Tony. They inspired each other.

He had the heavy, smooth muscles of a well-fed swimmer. Big legs, barrel neck, a stomach the rest of us could have used for body armor. He smiled a lot, too.

And he read things we didn't read. Marvel comics. The Incredible Hulk. He admired the Hulk's body, and he envied his lack of abstraction. Calvin had a whole philosophy built around it. It struck him as the one true freedom.

Vietnamese lived under the bridge with us. In the back where the bank sloped up and there wasn't much headroom. But they were short.

Courteous people. They were unobtrusive and made a special effort not to attract our attention. But they couldn't help being Vietnamese, and we were suspicious of them. We hung a line of ponchos at our back so they couldn't see in.

A puppy lived with us, too. A clumsier animal you never saw. He was so young he still had to squat down. Our home was his home, and it was a kennel.

Brown and lumpy with a loose potbelly, Mudball crashed happily around, investigating the same mysteries every time he passed. It was like living with an out-of-control potato.

Mudball belonged to Calvin, and Calvin was the center of Mudball's day. Whenever Calvin left the area, even just to go to the latrine, Mudball went berserk with loneliness. He would hurl himself against his string until he lay in a mournful heap.

Then Cal would come back, and the puppy would dance on his tail with gladness. And Cal would be just as glad.

One morning Mudball got loose and backed through the ponchos to a new world. A place he'd never suspected, with people he'd never seen. He fumbled his way over to the cooking fire. A middle-aged gentleman picked him up and gave him a little dish of food. It was the first time Mudball stopped thinking about Cal.

Meanwhile Cal finished his own stew and stepped outside. He didn't hear any mournful whimperings. And he didn't hear any joyful scampering when he came back in.

He looked back outside, and he looked by the river. The more he looked, the more frantic he got. And the more we backed out of the way of his big, muscle-man body.

It was a slow morning on the other side of the ponchos. Cool back there. Vietnamese squatted near the fire, eating and laughing softly. Playing with their kids. Napping.

Then Calvin burst in like a rocket through stained glass.

Into brown people dodging through scorching yellow smoke. Burning hair and searing flesh. Like a napalmed orphanage. His

154

face stung. And at the center a middle-aged gentleman was dan-
gling a plump carcass into a fire. Holding its thin tail.

"MUDBALL. They're cooking Mudball."

The middle-aged man didn't speak English, but he was no fool. He smiled and held the corpse out to Calvin.

Calvin wasn't ready for that. He stopped like he'd seen a recruiting sergeant. Before he could get started again, a fat brown four-legged figure dashed from behind a bedroll and smashed into a bucket.

The middle-aged man went back to scorching his rat. When it was clean, he chopped it into the stew.

We talked about it for days. Whenever rat hair acid smoke drifted to our side of the ponchos, somebody would ask after the puppy. Maybe he was with the Vietnamese?

And Mudball really would be with the Vietnamese. He liked the enchanted, smoky place on the other side of the ponchos where the middle-aged gentleman scratched his ear and the old lady fed him rat entrails from a C-ration can.

Cal got so disgusted he spent his evenings fuming around in the dark, springing traps. It never worked, though. Every morning the gentleman scorched a rat anyway. The smell would burn its way over into our area, and somebody would ask after Mudball. And the rest of us would shout our opinions.

"MUDBALL. THEY'RE COOKING MUDBALL."

It made breakfast more cheerful.

"They'll eat a dog, you know."

■ LAST DAY PATROL

In the daytime we went where we pleased and did as we chose, with no one to tell us no. We threw back the logs and charged onto the river. Knights with all America at our backs: artillery and air strikes. Infantry and armor and decency. It was our joy.

But when we came back, we came back alone. Nobody to meet us. No troupes of gaily clad damsels. No musicians. No jugglers. We left the dancing colors and soft smells and strange music out on the river. Out where we had spent the day chasing the shadows of a drab enemy. An enemy sent to bind that gaudy land in the gray fabric of its own short will. An enemy to innocence.

But one day was different. Somebody was waiting for us when we came back. Trim. Erect. Dark against the yellow bank. An officer was talking to Sergeant Stamford. I lost sight of them as we tied up under the dock.

The infantry scrambled out first, rattling weapons and bumping their helmets. Then I climbed up, and Short and Frank and the guy from South Carolina came over from the bridge. The captain had good news. No more day patrols. He wanted to tell us himself.

I'd never thought I was in danger on the river. I'd always thought the risk out there was Charlie's. It was he that hid from us.

From that day on, we just puttered our beautiful boats around the shadows under the bridge, forgetting we had ever known how to fight.

Compassion at a distance. We gave up so much. Those colonels and captains sitting on the bank couldn't have known how good we were.

But it was something else, too. It was body counts. How we kept score. Pull us out of combat. Leave fewer bodies on the river and we might win this war yet. That captain didn't care about saving our lives. He was just shaving points.

Thing was, Charlie didn't care about bodies. He kept tally by the territory he controlled and the commerce he wrecked.

■ PX

PX's infested the countryside. Places you couldn't go without air cover you could find a PX. So much normality so far from home.

One was down the main supply route from our bridge.

Two-lane blacktop through the silver-green countryside. Right to the door. And Calvin Rose wanted a camera.

Inside they were stacked like racks of produce. Calvin rolled them in his beefy hands, pressing shutters, working lenses, and playing with light meters. Buried in that pile was the one camera that had been built for Calvin. And his hands found it. All dark knobs and hidden switches. Solid and quick and black as Charlie's heart. A Nikon X.

He had seen all the beautiful and touching images brought home from Vietnam and multiplied endlessly by *Time* and *Look* and in hundreds of local papers. And he'd seen other things. Things correspondents never got near. He knew that his pictures would be better than theirs. And that his pictures could make him somebody other than Sergeant Rose.

And something else. The big bias. All those prisoners being shot in the head. His pictures would be different.

So many Americans carried cameras into combat that the enemy must have thought they were standard issue. The first war fought by tourists.

Calvin paid with orange paper. Military payment certificates. The army wouldn't give us greenbacks. MPCs didn't look like money. They were smaller and more colorful. They looked like the certificates that fall out of cereal boxes.

Fake payment for a war we were pretending to fight.

■ LOI

I think it was Loi's best outfit. Black slacks and a dull shirt. Drab. She wore it every day.

Loi was our servant. She cleaned under the bridge, arranged our boots, made our cots, and swept the dirt floor. Not much, really. But we didn't have much. And we didn't pay much, either. A buck or two a week. Everybody but me. I didn't pay at all. I made my own cot, straightened the mosquito net, and I didn't care which way my boots faced.

Servants embarrassed me. I'd seen too many back home.

But Loi wasn't embarrassed. She had a good heart and a sweet disposition and none of my sense of democracy. They paid her top scrip, and she meant to earn it. She cleaned like she was paying us for the chance. The rest of the time she sat alert, as Orientals do, waiting for a scrap of paper to drift by or for someone to take off his boots or for somebody to get up from his cot. Then she would stoop and straighten on the wing. Wherever there was mess.

I was messy. And I was sure I wouldn't pay. She'd smile and giggle and arrange my boots. I'd smile and laugh and refuse to pay. We had a cheerful relationship.

But unstable. Seven paying. Eight getting tidied. The books didn't balance, and after a while, the others mentioned it. I had to hire her. On the promise she wouldn't clean for me.

But of course she did. And she rubbed it in. She made my area sparkle.

Loi was medium height and thin, flat chested in the way of Vietnamese girls raised without a lot of protein. About seventeen. My sister's age. If things had been different, she would have been into dating and push-up bras and boys with fast cars. But as it was, she hung around a military encampment.

We could have done pretty much as we wanted with her, I suppose. But we never tried. She was just there to clean and to be friends.

Or so I thought until the day she took Frank and me home. To a house pressed between other houses and all of them run together into a single adlibbed structure. To old signs and sheets of tin.

158

Walls of secondhand building material like something put together by kids. A condo clubhouse along the side of the road.

We spun up. Gravel spat on tin, and her father stepped out. Mid-forties. Smiling. An old-fashioned gentleman.

He invited us in with gestures. We all spoke gesture.

It was as neat as Loi kept our place. And for the same reason. They didn't have anything, either.

Except a couple of cold Buds, which he gave to us. They must have been expensive for him. He couldn't have gotten them at the PX. It was a waste, really. I couldn't enjoy mine. I was too worried about battery acid.

At the time, I thought he just wanted to meet the people who paid his daughter. Now I think it was something more.

He didn't know what was coming for his country, but he could see that what was happening was no good. Invaded by one group of foreigners and occupied by another. He wanted Loi out of there. He wanted her to have what my sisters had. And he was trying to arrange it for her.

". . . modest. Work hard. Marry GI."

Only it never had a chance of working. When we left there, we left Loi.

It was a shame. Loi was so good. She would have made an excellent wife. Quiet, conscientious, and probably filled with marital wisdom from an aunt. But she had bad advice. All we could see was the prim virgin buzzing around the place. Untouchable. American girls knew better. They dressed like tramps and held their real worth to themselves. Fantasy. Loi just showed us who she was. Cheerful. Hardworking. Respectable. He counted on us to see the value in her. But we weren't looking for that kind of value.

■ LATRINE

We had a two-holer about fifty meters down river. Somebody came by periodically and dumped in lime, but from the smell you would have thought there were at least five holes in there. Nobody wanted to spend any more time inside than he had to.

The trick was to put off your visits until the pressure had built up so much that you could blast yourself clean without waiting. Ripper used to claim he could take a breath, step inside, close the door, drop his pants, pressure-flush his system, wipe, and be out of there without ever inhaling.

Frank told us he saved time by wiping before he went in.

One day the doors slammed open and Cal and an Arvin flew out like escaping apes, gasping and pointing at each other.

"Squatting. I tell you the son of a bitch was squatting in there. Goddamn filthiest thing I ever saw. People got to sit on that seat and there he was, a line of turds sliding down the hole like handkerchiefs out of a magician's hat. My ass snapped shut so quick it was like somebody'd lit my balls. Now I've got to go back in there to finish up. Shit."

A couple of nights later, when we'd all had a little to drink, the Arvin lieutenant came by. So courteous he could hardly get his question out. But we understood. He wanted to know whether we all sat in the latrine. It seemed so . . . unclean.

In the end, we compromised. They squatted over the left. We sat on the right.

Didn't work, though. Nobody was willing to hop around crosslegged, waiting for somebody to leave, when there was an empty seat on the other side.

The Arvins gave up the arrangement before we did. They took to going in whichever door they wanted and positioning themselves as they pleased. And we began imagining footprints everywhere, piled like leaves fallen on the seats. None of us wanted to sit anymore and we all became secret squatters. Except when somebody was in there with us.

160   It was a new trick for us, squatting, feet apart, aiming at articu-

lated cones heaped almost to our asses like immense lime-sugared pastries floating in a custardy liquid. Processed American food. Sweet beef. Proud corn and wheat whispering in the prairie sun. Fat chickens and boisterous hogs and peaches heavy on southern trees. That great Mississippi of food and treasure had come to the end of the line.

■ CLASS PROJECT

B undles of letters the size of shoe boxes lay on my bunk. Some kind of mistake. The mail for a platoon. A platoon probably had mine. But they were addressed to me. Every one of them. A couple from my dad. One about politics from a person I'd never met. And about forty written by childish hands:

"Mrs. Brentnall is making me rite this. You are the sojer we rite too."

The guys had been waiting for me to get back.

"I can't go to reses till I am don this."

"So what IS that shit? You must have fifty-sixty letters there." The mail was turning into a social liability.

". . . a sister named mary alice and the last privit we wrote to died and we never got to meet him at all."

"Some kind of service, isn't it? You signed up for that shit, didn't you?"
"I'm somebody's class project."
"Well, I only got two God DAMN letters, and Ripoli over there didn't get none. So tell them God DAMN class projects to be God DAMN careful about who they go sending six pounds of mother FUCKING mail to."
All that mail and no contact. Those kids didn't know me. Mrs. Brentnall might as well have sent their spelling tests.
So many sunlit kids squirming through grade school in Atlanta, struggling with hard desks, never moving all day without permission. Everything by the numbers. Even letters to a dead soldier. And do it again.
The army run by women. I could remember it better than Basic.

Georgia, Georgia, the whole day through,
Just an old sweet song keeps Georgia on my mind.

162   On balance I would rather have been where I was.

■ KID STEALING FOOD

More people lived outside the bridge than stayed under it with us. A hundred meters down the road, fifty or so Vietnamese squatted around little fires at night and chatted and argued during the day. People who had walked to us barefoot and broke, seeking forlorn comfort in our nearness.

In dry weather they slept under the stars. During the rains they crouched beneath strips of plastic and old pieces of lumber, more miserable than their first ancestors sheltering in hollow trees. They didn't eat as well, either, living off government rice and what small animals they could catch. Not starving but hungry in a land that had been overflowing before the nighttime cancer of invasion came to eat at the nation. Everywhere the enemy made war on food.

It was a tedious life. They stuck with it because it seemed safe. The places they had left were hostage to struggles not their own. Foreign soldiers moved through those places, sometimes killing an Arvin or an American or a government sympathizer and then scattering back into the countryside, no help against the retribution they had called down. Chiefs who closed their villages to the killers were found sleeping in blood the next morning, their throats cut.

The refugees stayed with us at Phu Cuong, not growing rice, building nothing, and thinking themselves well off near men who didn't want their food, didn't like their women, and didn't care about the correctness of their politics. Men who by and large ignored them.

For the most part they stuck to themselves. We were too big and rich. And too well armed. Or maybe we just smelled bad from all the protein we ate.

Only the kids came to visit and they not very often. Only when their mothers weren't looking. Then they were off like escaping popcorn to roll under the bridge with the sinister Americans and the tasty smells of rat. It was better than the movies.

One kid made it by more than the others. Quick, with an animated face, he always wore the same gray pants and checked shirt. He strutted in with the arrogance of a black ten-year-old arriving late to the fourth grade. We'd talk pidgin, his white teeth gleaming in the shadows of his dusty face. At the end he always grabbed a can of C's.

"Hey, GI, you give me, yes? You good GI. Number one soldier."
And run out with it before I could answer.
I never saw him eat the stuff, just run away with it.

> I'm awful cold and hungry, sir,
> My clothes are torn and thin
> I wander about from place to place
> My daily bread to win.

No sweat. We had more.

No sweat until the morning Sergeant Stamford reached under his bunk and came up bare. A cardboard crate of C's had been there when he went to bed.

None of us had it, and none of us admitted to knowing who did. We'd all had our fill of the stuff, anyway. Either somebody had sold it to the Gooks or we'd been overrun in our sleep. Like the village chiefs.

Nobody confessed to having sold it, so somebody must have gotten in.

I moved closer to the big steel wrench on the wall while Sergeant Stamford stepped up to the dusty mob outside. They didn't know about his food. Hadn't taken it, didn't know who had, hadn't seen anybody take it, and didn't know anybody except us who looked especially well fed.

The next time it might be weapons, and we didn't know who to blame. It could have been anybody. It could have been Loi. It could have been Ha. Especially Ha. No one who wasn't an American spent as much time with us as Ha. He knew where everything was, and he knew where we were.

The morning wore into afternoon. Tony and Frank went somewhere in a jeep. A big green tanker backed down to the river and gassed up our boats. Short and I swam and sunned ourselves on the dock. About 4:00 we walked back up to the bridge. He lay down and I sat on a footlocker, writing letters. I was licking an envelope when the kid with the checked shirt and the gray pants strutted by, carrying an empty cardboard crate of C rations down to the trash burner.

I shook Sergeant Stamford. He stepped out into the sun but nobody was there. Before I understood what was happening he was up the hill and back with the kid.

"This the one?"

The kid stood there calm, looking at me. He never said a thing.

> And I am helping Mother, sir,
> As I journey on my way.

I've never had much luck with remembering faces. The more I thought on it, the less I was sure who I was looking at. I couldn't confirm it.

The kid strutted away. He never changed expression.

Back under the bridge I felt rotten.

The kid didn't visit us after that, but mornings, sometimes, I would see him with the wolfhounds across the river. I pulled over there, once, before breakfast.

He was open for business. A full-service dope supply house: roach clips, papers, matches. He had it all.

He never blinked when he saw me. Just kept going from man to man, quoting prices on little packages of grass and bundles of paper. Offered some to me but I didn't want it. He shrugged and swaggered away. When he was gone, one of the wolfhounds looked at me.

"That kid know you? He sure quoted you a high price."

> So never mind, sir, how I look,
> Don't look at me and frown,
> I sell the morning papers, sir,
> My name is Jimmie Brown.

B right as it was outside, it was dim under the bridge and it took an effort to make out Sergeant Stamford's calm dark face.

"Got the word from Cu Chi, gentlemen. Sappers been spotted on the Trail above Ban Phon.

"Think they're so damn safe they're moving down as a unit. Like they're back home. Hell. They're *safer* than back home. In Hanoi they might get bombed.

"Due at the border in about two weeks. And over here when they're damn good and ready."

It seemed like we could hear them from where we sat. Hordes of them. Streams of sappers surging down the Trail. A river of enemies moving at night, shrouded by the trees. Tiptoeing through the dark places. Stepping around listening devices and stepping over land mines. Coming by bicycle and by truck and by oxcart and by elephant and on foot. A giant fester spilling poison into the body of a dying nation.

A torrent of sappers.

"When we going out and stop them?"

"You gentlemen know the rules."

■ GUNSHIPS

THE WATCHES OF THE NIGHT

Tied to the log boom, away from the lights, we could watch the moving sky, the dark river and the circlet of darker logs. And sometimes other things.

Bright neon threads hanging straight from the sky. Crystal red lines dancing on the night. Moving and blinking in a rhythm I could not grasp. They looked solid, like rods. And they didn't fade out at the top. Just stopped. Like they'd gotten to where they were going. They must have been thousands of feet long, they were so far away.

I had no idea what to make of them.

"Gunships."

As soon as Short said it, I knew he was right. AC-47s flying in slow circles. Three General Electric M61 gattling guns. Eighteen barrels. Eighteen thousand rounds per minute. Twenty percent red tracers. So many it didn't look like bullets at all. Just a thin pencil of sparkling ruby light. Beautiful beams of death. They'd found Charlie.

"God help him."

■ PHANTOM TRUCK TIRE

Tony and Calvin had been circling each other for hours.

". . . matter what you think, it was in the middle of the road. I stopped and looked right at it."

"You didn't see shit. That road doesn't even go to Cu Chi."

"So who wants to drive that same old main supply route all the time, anyway? You can't open up your mind doing shit like that."

"Charlies all over the road. You can't drive out there at night."

"It wasn't even getting dark when I left Cu Chi. It just got dark before I got back here. Besides, Charlie doesn't bother me. That's what I've been taking lessons for."

"You're taking mind control lessons to keep Charlie away from you?"

"It's working, isn't it?"

"You tell me you almost ran into a truck tire full of explosives and you think it's working?"

Calvin turned his back in rhetorical triumph. Tony didn't notice. He just answered the back. Ears work both ways.

"I'm telling you, I saw what I saw. It was a bright night and I was late and I was going fast. Got to that bend where the road crosses the canal and . . . "

"And you had this hallucination."

". . . and there's these high bushes on the left."

"I've seen them. Just this morning, as a matter of fact. Got out and walked all around. Looked in the bushes and looked in the dust for scrape marks. Even checked the road for bomb craters. Couldn't find any tires. Couldn't find any SIGN of any tires."

Cal had turned back around.

"The moon was up and shadows from those bushes were on the road. Don't like driving through shadows. I slowed down. Something snapped out at me and I hit the brakes and skidded to the right. I was crossways in the road by the time I stopped. Almost in the canal. And right next to a truck tire. Big. Probably a deuce-and-a-half. And packed with explosives. Wires running all over the place. You never heard an engine start so noisy. I didn't want to touch that tire or go into the canal, either. Took a lot of fancy steering. I kept thinking about the tire, trying to keep it from blowing up. Really using my mind control."

"Mind control? You learned how to start your engine in jeep school."

"Damn straight, it was mind control. I spotted that tire when I needed to, didn't I? I stopped the jeep without hitting it, didn't I? And I didn't go into . . . "

"Why didn't you just drive right by? You stopped at the only place in the whole world that was between that tire and the canal. Those people are taking your money, Tony."

". . . and I got out of there without anybody blowing the tire up."

"You don't need mind control, you need brain control."

"If it wasn't for my mind control you know what you'd be doing this morning? You'd be requisitioning yourself a new jeep and a new corporal."

"If it wasn't for your God damn mind control, I'd be asleep.

"And if I did need a new corporal, I'd get me one with a mind to control. They've got a box for that, you know. Right there on DD form 1472 where you can check what kind of mind you want in your new corporal. I got in a hurry last time and left it blank. Supply didn't know what to send, so they improvised. And look what I got. Next time I'm going to be more specific.

"Phantom God damn truck tire. It's all been a lesson to me."

"You would have seen it, too."

"I sure as hell looked. I stumbled around on my hands and knees, looking. And no tire. No sign of nothing. Want to know what I think? I think there never was any PHANTOM GOD DAMN TRUCK TIRE out there."

"Don't matter what you think. It was in the middle of the road. I stopped and looked right at it."

"You didn't see shit. That road doesn't even go to Cu Chi."

"So who wants to drive the same old main supply route all the time, anyway? You can't open up your mind doing shit like that. . . . "

■ TAKING WATER

THE WATCHES OF THE NIGHT

More war stories in the dark.

"Came over thinking I'd be driving a boat but showed up at the wrong time and got attached to a company of grunts humping around in the boonies. TDY, they called it. Temporary duty. Nobody'd say how long you had to be out on patrol before the duty became permanent. Seemed to me it might happen when you left the base camp. I'd heard stories.

"I was the newest guy out there. Cherry Boy, they called me. 'Don't walk next to Cherry Boy. Cherry Boys get into things and blow up.'

"Nothing happened the first few days. We walked across the dry parts and slogged through the wet, setting up our perimeter in the afternoons and pulling it back down in the mornings while I tried to look like infantry.

"Then one afternoon we camped on a rise next to a canal. On the other side was a low hill. Toward evening they sent me down for some water. Outside the wire.

"I made one trip, and then I went back for more, arms full of webbing and canteens. I muffled the noise as best I could, but it was dark and I snapped brush sometimes. And the canteens made hollow sounds when they bumped together. At the canal I made more noise, looking for the way down. But the way down found me first. Feet shot out on the wet mud, and I was waist deep with a noise like a garbage truck rolling over.

"By then it was dark. I'd fill a canteen and then I'd listen for other sounds. After a while I heard some. A rustle of clothing and a snap of twigs on the wrong side the canal. Made my neck prickle. I was trying to figure out what to do when the whole bank erupted with Green Tracers.

"GREEN TRACERS.

"Enemy tracers like big green fists. Coming straight for me. But they missed. Just throbbed over my head and kept on going, vibrating toward camp.

"It was like the night infiltration course in Basic. And just as
scary.

"Right then the far side seemed a lot safer than where I was. So I stumbled over and flattened myself on it. There was no way back to camp. I'd grab a green bullet with my ass. Or I'd catch a red one in the teeth as soon as my buddies heard me coming.

"When the green bullets tapered off, the red ones blasted from behind and I was back across the canal, hugging the American bank. Then a green volley and across again. It kept up all night while I churned a path across the bottom of the canal. Nobody came near me. All that shooting kept them away.

"The firing finally stopped, morning came, and I walked back to camp with an armload of canteens. I hadn't thought about them since I'd first heard enemy moving in the brush. But they were still on my arms when the sun came up.

"Nobody ever called me Cherry Boy again."

■ CUTTING LOOSE

S on of a bitch."
    Short killed the engines, and the logs pulled back into a curve. Dragging us with them.

We'd spent the night tied to the log booms. We did that, sometimes. Before the army put a stop to it. Dangerous, they said. But it was safer than being in with the grenades.

Now we were hung up. Rope in the prop.

Short stepped onto a log. Then he turned and squatted, feeling under the boat like he was delivering a calf.

"Tighter'n Vietnamese snatch. Take me all morning."

Wasn't room enough on that log for both of us, so I just waited.

"No sweat. Got me a good book here. Just stretch out on these hatches and listen to you splash."

"Okay, good book. Too bad you don't have a good knife."

"Had one, but a sergeant back at Cu Chi found it. Good one, too. Cut the wings off a fly. Slice that rope so easy you'd think you were still waving it through the water. Careful you didn't cut the prop off."

"Well, I'll just cut the prop off with this Coke can here."

Army wouldn't let us have knives. Just M16s and bayonets and percussion grenades and fragmentation grenades and phosphorous grenades and rifle grenades and machine guns. But a jackknife was too dangerous.

So we used a ragged Coke can and chewed our way free, gnawing through a tangled rope like a rat through a hawser. And almost as fast.

Ragged Coke cans weren't legal either. They were garbage, and we kept ours hidden. It could have gotten policed up.

Then:

"Son of a bitch. Grab on, GRAB ON." The boat rocked free and was drifting away.

"You could lose an arm doing this."

"Hang on while I unwind the prop." Brown fibers floated up. Then:

"Let's get the hell out of here."

172   I never wanted to get attacked out there.

■ UPPER-CLASS WOMEN

It was smoky under the bridge. Pungent with burning hair while dusty shapes glided through the haze. Lean Vietnamese men and their dusty, flat-faced women clutching after bustling children. They were all the Vietnamese in the world, to us. The background of our lives. As ordinary as workers in some steaming kitchen.

But there were others. Once, while I was wiping the breakfast grease from my teeth, a sound filtered in. Musical and modulated laughter like a wind chime. Elegant laughter. Finishing-school laughter.

I straightened my fatigues, pulled on a pair of flip-flops, and went to see.

They stood just off the road. Six or eight high-collared slit dresses. Magenta and gold and scarlet and emerald. Pale thighs. Black hair sparkling over hips as they rustled about, beautiful as hummingbirds.

> I, I love the colorful clothes she wears,
> And the way the sunlight plays upon her hair.
> I hear the sound of a gentle word,
> On the wind that lifts her perfume through the air.

Round hips and round faces and liquid breasts. Too beautiful for Vietnamese.

Good nutrition, mainly. Rich children grew up taller and more womanly. But it was more.

Their skin wasn't dusty and their faces were round. And their noses stuck out and their cheeks curved back to their ears. The women we knew were so flat-faced they would have drowned if they'd slept on their backs in the rain.

These bright visitors were something else. Part . . . French. An honor to both parents.

I hadn't expected the perfume.

Or their legs flashing in the sun, their soft smiles meant for me, calling me over.

Close my eyes,
She's somehow closer now,
Softly smile,
I know she must be kind.

But it didn't come to anything. They just kept talking and laughing. Didn't even pull in on themselves. Eyes glancing off me on the way to more profitable sights. Nothing they would ever commit to long-term memory.

I felt like an arctic wolf stalking a circle of musk oxen. Hungry. On the outside.

It went like that until a daytime captain drove them away in a drab army bus. I never saw them again.

It occurred to me later that maybe they weren't rich after all. Maybe they worked for a living like everybody else.

■ FRANK'S GIRLFRIEND

W hat you need is a girlfriend."

Frank bustled around in the hard yellow light.

"I've got a girlfriend. What I need is to be with her."

"No, I mean here. Here. You need a girl where you are now."

The thing was, he was right. But there weren't any girls where I was then. Girls were all back in the World. Except doughnut dollies, and who wanted to pay for one of them?

"Get yourself one over in the village there, like . . . "

"Don't want a . . . "

". . . visit mine at home. Got her own room. Real comfortable. King-size mattress. Rugs all around. And some number one dope. We play the radio and she tells me about her family up north and I tell her what it's like back in the world. Sometimes I stay all night."

"What about her parents? What do . . . ?"

"Oh, they don't care. They're up north. She escaped down here with the other girls. They've all got their own rooms."

"Frank, you've found a . . . "

"Don't call her that. She loves me and I get her every time. She doesn't care about any of those others. Come on and find one yourself."

"So what's all this going to cost me?" I didn't want to get in over my head.

Not much, as it turned out. Not from the prices Frank quoted. Not by the experience. Not by the night. So cheap I could have stayed a week for a can of C's. But Frank advised against paying that way.

"Stamford counts the damn things."

And I was still concerned.

"The Chinese clap. They'll put me on that island they've got some damn place and tell my parents I was found missing."

"Who told you about that Chinese clap shit? Some sergeant? What does a sergeant know about clap? Sergeant don't know fucking from shit, man. They're SERGEANTS. Got no romance, for crap's sake. Think a tit's full of beer and a pussy's just a new recruit.

"You know why so many sergeants wear glasses? Because they

never get any relief. Pressure backs up and makes them go blind. Then they get assigned to the inspector general."

Maybe, but I couldn't see gambling on it.

I woke up the next morning when Short came back from patrol. Frank was still gone.

We cooked a pot of C's for breakfast.

■ DOUGHNUT DOLLIES

You got to see them."
　　The word came by wolfhound. Two guys from the platoon
　　across the river. So excited they talked over each other.

"Red Cross truck just got here this morning. Some good stuff."

I'd never met a doughnut dolly. But I'd heard stories.

"Give you some relief after this place. Fuck over your brain to hang around here too long. Get to thinking everybody in the world eats out of cans, and chicks are all short and dusty. And flat like they'd been cooked on a skillet and wear floppy pants and eat the wrong parts of a fish."

"Shit, chicks here look so much like boys you could make the big switch just from humping on one. Then go home and start hanging out at the wrong bars."

Frank sat up on his bunk.

"What the hell you trying to . . . ?"

"I said you sure need a big switch to handle one of these . . . "

"Damn straight you do."

Frank sank back down.

"Spent the morning with them doughnut dollies. They won't be forgetting me for a while, neither, I can tell you that."

". . . whoo hee. Long legs and big shoulders. Stuff I'd forgot all about. And wait till you get a load of the buttons stretching on their shirts. Man, I thought they'd bust loose. . . . "

". . . buttons? You ought to get a load of when they take their shirts off. Big pink nipples jumping in the air. America come to us. . . . "

". . . you should go on down. Get yourself CONUS fucked right back of the collection cans. Ain't got nowhere else to spend your money over here. . . . "

". . . a hundred dollars. . . . "

". . . no point to dickering, neither. Don't make no difference whether she's fat or ugly or got blood running down her legs, it's going to cost you one hundred bucks. . . . "

". . . like dealing with trappers. When beaver's scarce, them that are carrying the pelts sets the price. . . . "

". . . my old buddy Harry's the only one I ever know who got it　177 for less. But it didn't do him no good. Got blowed away the next morning. . . . "

". . . told everybody he had a twelve-inch dick. 'I've got it certified. You want to see a affidavit? Seven and one-half to eight inches round, too. . . . "

". . . well, they drew straws for it. Long straw was so embarrassed when she found out the truth she wouldn't tell nobody. Didn't want her friends to know how bad she'd been screwed. Second one didn't tell neither. Got through six of them before he gave out. . . . "

". . . next day was Tet. If he hadn't of been so wore out he might not have tried to take cover behind that fence."

What the girls got out of it, besides rich, was a year-long fling, a tour of the agony of a dying nation, and a trip to the zoo to toss food at the bears.

But who's to say the bears didn't enjoy it?

Afternoon in the last week in September and I was at the bottom of a velvet well, floating on a still pool of darkness, listening to the voices above. Yanking at me. Until I was snatched awake into the hard world of a dying South Vietnam, where I didn't want to be.

We'd all been jerked awake. Except for Tony, and he wasn't getting much rest. Thrashing and yelling like he was, he might have been trying to sleep on a griddle.

Cal had him by the shoulders.

"Wake up. It's just a dream.

"Wake up."

But Tony didn't wake up any easier than I had.

"Walk around. It was just a dream."

"It wasn't a dream."

"You'll forget it."

"It was real, damn it. Here. This bridge. They're going to hit it. I saw it."

"Who is? Who's going to hit the bridge?"

"Those sappers, damn it. Who do you think? I've seen it."

"So tell the captain when he comes out. Have it stopped."

"I told you, I've seen it. It's like it already happened. Captain can't stop it. . . . "

"Maybe we could find a colonel."

". . . and a lot of guys are going to get wasted."

"Who? Who are they?"

"Me? Will I be one?"

"How about me?"

"And me?"

"Damn you guys, how should I know? People were hanging all over the rail, facing the water. I couldn't see who they were."

"Us? Arvins?"

"Everybody. It was awful."

"Maybe we could put some money in a helmet. Those that are left could split. . . . "

"You bastard. I saw it. People are going to be killed."

"How about you? Were you up there on the rail?"   179

"I won't be here that night."

"You're always here."

"I won't be here then."

"Ain't nobody going to let you leave."

"Hang around November 5 and watch."

"November 5? That's when they're hitting the bridge?"

"And you. That's the night."

■ CLEARING THE AIR

THE WATCHES OF THE NIGHT

PLSSSH
    PLSSSH
        PLSSSH
"HEY YOU . . .
    BWWWAAAAMMM
        ". . . CAREFUL WITH THOSE . . .
            BWWWAAMMM
                ". . . GRENADES . . .
                    BWWWWAAAMMM
KLATTTatatattttt
    "IN THE BOAT. IT'S . . .
        THmmmp . . .
            THmmp . . .
                dottLLt . . . dotLtLtt . . . klatatt
"AROUND IN THE BOAT."
    And over the side.
    Plsss
B-BWWWWWWWAAAAAAAMMMMMMMMMMMAANNGGGGG

None of the frags touched us, but the boat leaked from then on.

Before the water quit vibrating, Short had his rifle and was on the pier. I jumped up behind, but he beat me to the bunker. I guess he'd seen people killed by grenades. I hadn't, then.

The place was as brightly lit and as vulnerable looking as a phone booth at night. Short had an Arvin shoved down into a corner. He had his rifle to his head, and three other people shrank back into the sandbags.

My God, it's going to be an execution. There's going to be pictures on the cover of *Time,* and Short's going to be famous.

". . . BLOW YOU FUCKIN AWAY, YOU BICK?"

Arvin looked apologetic.

> Well here I sit high gettin' ideas
> Ain't nothing but a fool would live like this
> Out all night and runnin' wild
> My woman sittin' home with a month-old child.

But before he fired, Short found an open baggy on the table. And half a bottle of scotch propped on a sandbag.

Arvin kept trying to explain.

> Just sittin' around drinkin' with the rest of the guys,
> Six rounds bought and I bought five . . .

Short stomped the grass into the floor.

"You got any more of this shit?"

Arvin pointed to the pocket on his flak jacket. Short threw the jacket into the river.

Then he found some more in an ammo box. The whole brick went into the water along with three crates of grenades and all the ammunition in the bunker. He smashed the scotch against number three pier across the way. When the place was cleaned out, he wheeled back on the Arvin.

"Kneel down, cherry mother fucker." The Arvin had a wild look but there was nowhere to run. When Short kicked the back of his knees, he sank down. Even then I don't think he believed he would pull the trigger.

But Short did pull it, and the Arvin collapsed against the table.

CLICK

"Next time, cherry mother fucker, I'll have a ROUND IN THE CHAMBER. YOU BICK, YOU BASTARD?"

When we left, Arvin was still apologizing.

> DANG ME,
> DANG ME,
> They ought-ta take a rope and hang me
> High from the highest tree,
> Woman would you weep for me!

■ MORNING

Hot night on the river.

When your eyes are shut, every grenade lands in the boat.

Even when you sleep, distant explosions slam through the water and slap you in the spine. Ghost blasts, like biting into tin foil. Wraiths of burning wire.

Slow nights ragged with adrenaline.

By dawn it was over. The grenades had stopped, and the river had cooled.

The beautiful Song Saigon exulting beneath us. Morning mists hanging in rags over yellow water. No hurry. Nothing to do. We'd prop ourselves up, and then we'd lie back down.

Sun came with an easy gray light. The broad river stretched like a shining yellow road curving behind emerald trees on its way to forbidden cities while complicated green and silver inlays shimmered on its banks through the morning fog. And Frank and the guy from South Carolina had the next watch.

■ CLEARING PROP

It was a hot morning. It would be a hot day.

I woke several hours after dawn, my boat tied to the log boom where I'd moored it for night patrol. I cleared some rope from the props, punched on the motors and glided over to the dock. The water was a third low and falling. It was a long step up.

An officer I did not know jumped down into the boat. He'd studied the way engineering officers looked: medium height, wiry, white walls with a shock of nut-colored hair on top. Competent, confident, and looking for combat experience.

Captain Whipsinger. A sniper could have picked him out at four hundred meters.

Then Sergeant Stamford jumped on. And then Tubb. I made them put on life jackets. It was my boat.

One last day patrol. We swarmed up the river, trailing ribbons of yellow froth, and nobody ever consulted me as to where. I could have been the engine room attendant.

"All ahead two-thirds, Mr. Sprocket."

"Aye aye, sir."

The captain had a map. Tubb was waving to the left. After a while we came to the square mouth of an irrigation canal carved into the bank.

We went in. It was wide enough. I could turn the boat in there. Even if the canal narrowed, I could back out.

Slow. A fraction of our speed on the open river ("All ahead slow, Mr. Sprocket"). Fast enough for a canal, though. The yellow bubbles drifted behind us.

I'd never been in that canal before. I couldn't tell its depth from the glossy yellow surface we slid over. But Frank had been there. He was our guide. Not much for him to point out, though. The yellow banks rose higher than we could see.

Navigation didn't require much effort. It was like trying to find your way through a tunnel: only two directions were implicated, and we'd already used up one.

We turned back when the water was filled with stumps and reeds. We didn't have the clearance. Judging by the reaction, it was an important frustration. Captain Whipsinger took it hard. It was all Tubb's fault.

"You stupid SON OF A BITCH, you TOLD us you'd passed through here at low water."

"I did, GODDAMN it."

"You're starting to get a reputation for this kind of shit."

That was about as bad as Sergeant Stamford ever talked to anybody.

"God DAMN it. All I know is I came through there back in August."

"You should have looked up. When your brains are in your ASS-HOLE, you see things upside down."

It went on like that. Entertainment for me. Like when one of my sisters was in trouble.

"What if we'd gotten hung up in that shit? Charlie'd be rolling grenades down on us and we couldn't shoot back. Couldn't even see him over those mother fuckin banks. What we gonna do then? Tell the stumps to let us through because you said they aren't here?"

"SHEE-IT."

That was it. The last act it took to get us hung up. Like an incantation. The words weren't fairly out before the boat twanged with an elastic snap and lurched to the right. And stopped. Something in the props. Someone had to get it out. And it was my boat.

I slid off the back and the yellow water closed over my head.

> And we lived beneath the waves
> In our yellow submarines.
> We all live in a yellow submarine,
> Yellow Submarine,
> Yellow Submarine.

Heavy wire twisted all around.
"Comm wire in the prop and the rudder."

> Yellow Submarine,
> Yellow Submarine.

"Runs across the canal. We're anchored on both sides."
Back underwater the wire hadn't gotten any looser.

"Anybody got a knife?"

"You gotta be shitting me."

So it was dive and twist. Dive and twist.

> Yellow Submarine,
> Yellow Submarine.

Too tight to pull over the blades.

> Yellow Submarine,
> Yellow Submarine.

Looped and twisted in a double strand, hard against the shaft. But the prop would still turn, and I turned it, forcing it to unwind.

> Yellow Submarine,
> Yellow Submarine.

At last I backed the wire off. It snapped to the bottom like a bowstring, and we were out of there. As soon as I put water in the motor.

"All ahead full, Mr. Sprocket."

Tubb and the sergeant knew we spent a lot of time getting stuff out of props. That left Captain Whipsinger to think I was a hero. That was enough.

I never saw him again. Tubb never much wanted to talk about what had happened that morning. Sergeant Stamford wouldn't even admit that he'd been on the river. I've never found out what we were trying to do.

■ CLOSING LOG BOOM

I was contemplating the terrain inside a can of pork and beans—
one of my twelve favorite breakfasts—when the cough of a
jeep announced the arrival of a daytime officer bringing orders.
From now on, the log booms stayed closed and we stayed inside.
Frank went out to close them and I carried breakfast up top to
watch. The lieutenant was gone by the time I got there.

Tubb pulled those lines of dark logs as a needle tightens black
thread until he had sewn them to the shore.

When he was done, we were alone. An island separated from
Vietnam. The countryside beset us.

We had besieged ourselves under an open sky and in the midst of
an empty place. We lay within a magic ring, fashioned to keep the
enemy out, but since we alone believed in its magic, it served only
to keep us in.

> Can the circle
> Be unbroken
> By and by, Lord,
> By and by.

We were of no more consequence to the war. We went about our
little routines like scribes at the end of Rome, scribbling away while
Alaric gathered himself to bring down the world. Someday the bar-
barians would stand before us, too, with fire and steel. But not
today.

The time had been when we would throw back those logs and
stride the water like the whirlwind. The rivers had been ours, our
twin Chevy sixes snorting and pawing the yellow water like charg-
ers with their blood up. Whoever stood to say nay disputed with
our bullets and our grenades and the killer genies of our hidden
artillery and our screaming air power. Few could, and fewer dared.
Our spirit had been to find the enemy and hang up his guts for the
crows.

As long as we could do that thing, it was our river. We knew that,
and our enemy knew it—and his women knew it also. On that river
we cut straight through his heart.

187

■ 188
Phu
Cuong

But later, penned behind those logs, we no longer cared about the enemy. We wanted only to avoid him: to pierce the enchanted wooden ring and fly back to the World.

> There's a better
> Home a waiting
> in the sky, Lord,
> in the sky.

We moved through those days like creatures gliding in an aquarium, our eyes turned from the shadows gathering with hammers on the other side of the glass.

■ LOSING CONTACT

Sergeant Stamford kicked a sandbag.

"They're just over the border, gentlemen. Sappers.

"Intelligence followed them all the way from Hanoi. Down the Trail. Through Laos. Through Cambodia. Now they're thirty miles away, and they've lost them. Probably because there isn't a battalion there anymore. Just little groups of peasants drifting toward us in small boats. Twos and threes.

"Won't be a battalion again until they wash up with the garbage, down at the village. And every one of those mothers will have to pass under our bridge to get there. A hundred little inspection tours checking us out.

"Expect a lot of civilian traffic for the next few days, gentlemen."

"So, Sarge, we gonna start back up on the day patrols?"

"You gentlemen know the rules."

■ VOTING

The state of Georgia reached halfway around the world and found me under the bridge at Phu Cuong. A daytime officer dropped me off an absentee ballot along with the usual eccentric mail. It came in a long white envelope printed in red. So fat it felt like it was stuffed with newspaper. It wasn't, though. It was stuffed with a huge sheet of paper folded like a gargantuan road map. It unfolded to the size of a beach towel.

I spread the thing out on my mattress. The others kept their distance; it was a private occasion. But still, it was interesting to them, and they watched from the circle of their own bunks. Except for Sergeant Stamford, none of them had ever seen a ballot. None of them.

A referendum on the war. And they were all too young to vote.

Words covered the paper. Tiny, like names in the phone book. Right at the top was the main event. Humphrey vs. Nixon and the two of them vs. Wallace. Two contenders and a challenger. No champ.

Below was all a mystery. Candidates for state, county, and city positions. Regiments of names marching down the page. Down and down and down, through the lists of government offices. Down through legislators, judges, councilmen, and sheriffs and clerks and assessors and auditors and administrative assistants and coroners and cronies and hangers-on. Down through endless ranks of red letters.

An explosion of democracy.

Nobody back home could have known who those people were. Neither could I. So many politicians beckoning.

> Other arms reach out to me;
> Other eyes smile tenderly;
> Still in peaceful dreams I see
> The road heads back to you.
> Georgia, Georgia. . . .

But as it turned out, knowing the candidates wasn't important. Everybody ran unopposed. Hundreds and hundreds of offices and no choice. The real election had been the Democratic primary, and the Democrats hadn't sent me an absentee ballot. Uncle Ho would have recognized the procedure.

■ MACDEVITT

MacDevitt, Samuel H. Capt. 03, USAF. Born Charlotte, North Carolina, 20 July 1943. MIA, North Vietnam, 3 October 1968.

The clipping from the *Observer* was longer, but it didn't say anything more. He'd punched out over some place called Sontay up near the Red River. I never thought I'd hope somebody was in a North Vietnamese prison camp, but now I did.

He'd been two years ahead of me in Air Force ROTC. I'd always admired him. His uniforms hung in creased planes, while mine drooped like it was raining.

The rest of us would stand in cold lines under the winter sky while MacDevitt bobbed in and out, inspecting. Like some bright seabird darting through the surf. Of all of us, he was the easiest, the most comfortable as an officer. A soldier born to a family tradition.

He graduated a second lieutenant and went straight to flight school. I dropped out of ROTC that year. People with glasses don't get to fly.

My memories are mostly of uniforms out under the blue North Carolina skies. And as the years pass, I remember more of the sky and the blue uniforms and less of him.

Through a veil of tears, your vision disappears.

> Blue on blue
> Heartache on heartache
> Blue on blue
> Now that we are through
> Blue on blue
> Heartache on heartache.

■ WORLD SERIES

THE WATCHES OF THE NIGHT

". . . and now, direct from the world, THE ARMED FORCES RADIO AND TELEVISION NETWORK PRESENTS: *THE WORLD SERIES.*"

The Crackers took some when I was a kid, but the Braves shoved them aside when the major leagues moved to town. Milwaukee hadn't won much since it left Boston, and it never did anything in Atlanta, either. So it wasn't until Fort Leonard Wood that I cared about baseball. And then it was the Cards. Busch Stadium on weekends.

Are the 1968 Cardinals the best team in the history of organized ball? It's hard to compare.

This St. Louis club will never play the fabled Yankee teams of the fifties or the legendary Giants of the early twenties, so no one can know for sure. But here's how one reporter adds it up:

Consider Bob Gibson. An arm like the forward battery of the New Jersey, blasting pitches at hypersonic speeds past some of the best hitters ever to pick up a bat. He'll never go head to head with Grover Cleveland Alexander, and considering the lively modern balls, we can't even compare statistics. But my bet's on Gibson.

Then figure in Lou Brock. The smart money says he'll break Ty Cobb's base-stealing record this year. And even if he's not as good an all-around player as Cobb, when he gets to first, he's a run scored. No ball in the majors can catch him then. And Brock rotates through the batting order once every nine times, like a barrel on a gattling gun.

Then factor in Curt Flood. He roams the outfield like a mobile radar tracking station, plotting the trajectory of every incoming ball launched approximately toward the outfield. And then he picks that ball from the sky. Every time. Willie Mays? I watched Willie play for over ten years, and I don't know. But even if Willie were better, not a ball's been hit that can get past Flood, and that's enough for my money.

Gibson and Brock and Flood and about twenty other guys who'd be Hall of Famers on anybody else's club. Going up against the Cards is like going up against the United States Army. Other teams don't come to win.

So is this St. Louis club the greatest ever to put on uniforms? Too hard to compare. But when you talk to people who really know, when you talk to them late at night over a bottle of Jack Daniels, they'll admit that maybe it's so. That maybe the Cards are the greatest ever to lay wood on a ball.

But even if they're not, they're sure the best in the game today.

I watched the Cards all spring and into the summer. Then they'd gone on the road, and so had I. And now we were back together on my boat. Against the Tigers in the Series.

. . . had to call a sportswriter in Detroit to find out who those guys were. Nobody here had ever heard of them.

They're led by one Denny McLain. An old man, thirty-one and up against Gibson. Tiger Stadium keeps a cardiopulmonary unit on standby whenever McLain pitches.

With people like that against Gibson and Brock and Flood, this Series is gonna be a laugher. It won't go six games.

It almost didn't. The Cards won three of the first four and were leading 3 to 1 in the fifth. McClain had lost two, and Mickey Lolich, pitching for Detroit, was about to take the long march to the showers. Then Lou Brock came barreling into home. Standing up. He didn't slide. HE DIDN'T SLIDE. The greatest base runner in the world forgot to slide. Bill Freehan, the Detroit catcher with luck written in neon across his forehead, tagged Lou short of home. Detroit took it, 5 to 3.

Smarting from the previous day's loss, Lou Brock and the Cardinals returned to Busch Stadium, to Cardinal country and to hometown fans. The Cards only needed one and they'd already won three. . . .

The Tigers reached deep into that place where humiliated World Series pitchers go and found Denny McLain, who roared back out of retirement to hold the Cardinals to nine hits and one run while his teammates blasted through the St. Louis defense like paper targets. It was thirteen to one and the Series went into the seventh game.

Grenades dropped from the bridge like poisoned fruit while I lay on a boat, tied to a log boom on the dark side of the planet, listening to two American teams play for the championship of the world. The seventh game. Gibson was starting. I could see him in my radio, his sweaty black arm showering out strikes too fast for the human eye to spot. Streaks across the retina, painted over the infield like broken highway stripes. He struck out seven of the first twenty-three Tigers and allowed only three hits. No runs got by him at all.

Jim Northrup didn't get by him, either. Northrup hit a routine line drive to center which Flood tracked all the way. But the ball faded from Flood's screen as it passed a cluster of white-shirted fans. When he picked it back up, it was high. Curt Flood stepped back and tripped.

Northrup was safe on third. Two other Tigers made it home, and Lolich spent the rest of the day throwing junk.

Even the United States Army loses sometimes.

With Gibson and Flood and Brock on the same field, Mickey Lolich was chosen most valuable player. MICKEY LOLICH.

Gibson won two and would have taken a third except for someone else's error. Mickey Lolich, who almost didn't make it past the fifth, won two on errors. And the MVP. He didn't seem embarrassed about it, though.

"Everybody mentions heroes on the team, and Lolich has always been second or third best. Well, today was my day, and I'm glad it came."

Maybe. But he was still second best.

When dawn came, the warm water was lapping against the slick banks, and there was no justice in Mudville.

■ COMPARE WOUNDS

I woke up sweaty, my clothes chafing. Hot like a summer weekend back home. I spent a slow hour deciding to do nothing. Anybody wanting a letter from me would still want it tomorrow. With the log booms closed, the dock was the edge of our world. Going there was all the expedition we could mount. I went. The water was medium high and running downstream and I could hear the boats bumping against the pilings. Basting in the sun, I left wet silhouettes when I rolled over. A slow afternoon.

"Hey, GI. You come here log boom."

It was Ha capering along the logs. I stumbled to my feet to join him.

He was upstream a couple of hundred meters. I left my clothes on the dock and hopped along the bank, dancing on sharp things until I came to the still water behind pier number one and muddled my way into the river.

If Ha had been on a lake, I would have swum straight to him. No current to inconvenience my navigation. But he wasn't on a lake, and there was a current and I had to aim for a point upstream and try to wash down to where he was. I sighted on a dark palm tree far to the right and glanced up every couple of strokes. But it was a wide river, and my strokes weakened. My crisp line from the pier to Ha melted into a curve. I picked a new tree even further upriver and set out to drift into Ha from a different angle. It didn't work, either. I ran through a whole grove of palm trees while I washed downstream. There is no low point on a declining curve. In the end, I was struggling nearly straight upriver. Even when it seemed to me I was making progress, I was being sucked backward as fast as I could swim. The best I could hope for was to stay in one place for a while. In the end I rammed heel first onto the log boom. I couldn't miss it.

Ha was waiting. He'd calculated my arrival and gotten there a long time before I had. Ropey arms pulled me onto a log.

He clapped me on the back.

"How come you all time lay around? You got no job, eh?"

For a minute I was breathing too much to answer. Then:

"Why aren't you standing out in the sun? You AWOL?"

196

"Today, no. Today everybody forget Ha. New lieutenant. No bick Ha. You wait tomorrow. You see. Ha back at old place. Today Ha play in river. Like GI. No?"

Then he saw an ugly surgical scar on my chest. A memento of civilian days.

"What happened that?"

"VC."

I should have told him the truth. When somebody believes a joke, it turns into a lie. And you repent it.

"Ah, VC."

He sucked in his breath.

"Me also."

He pushed a finger into a dark purple hollow on his calf, his thumb on the other side where it had gone out. AK47.

"You—me—buddy. VC hurt me. VC hurt you too. Hurt you bad."

He got me in a big slippery embrace, his cheek to mine.

"Fuck VC. Hey, hey, FUCK VC, eh? FUCK VC."

(Ah, fuck, Ha.)

THE WATCHES OF THE NIGHT

H is whiskey wasn't so good, but it was sure better than any I'd brought. I gulped it like he was about to snatch it back. Under the light I could see him for what he was. A wolfhound. Gray skin. Sunken cheeks. Veins and tattoos and scars slatting over reptilian muscles.

A recruiting sergeant had found him shoveling coal at the bottom of the rattiest freighter on Lake Erie and had promised him a better life. He'd almost gotten it.

"Weren't no big thing.

"I was just setting up on this little piss ant of a hill, rolling a toke. Didn't have nothing to do and weren't anybody nowhere around. Just water, silver in all the fields. Then I saw, way off to one side, these black pajamas bobbing up and down. A little old mamasan stooping through her rice paddy, working straight toward me. Just me and her and all that water.

"I started thinking, the way we were, the two of us, what if I zapped her, who'd ever know?

"She never turned around or nothing, just kept sticking those bright little plants in the mud. And coming toward me.

"Just step and bend. Step and bend."

He poured three more fingers into a partially uncrumpled paper cup.

"Hell. My weapon was right there, and she wasn't offering much resistance, if you know what I mean, so I tried sighting her in. Didn't mean nothin by it. Just wanted to see what it looked like on her.

"Didn't change nothing. She just kept stepping and bending. Black on silver. We were like that for a long time. Her thinking about rice and me thinking about the best time to squeeze one off being just when she starts up from a bend and about how when I got back to the other guys I'm going to tell them how I saved this mamasan's life today when I had her in my sights but didn't squeeze the trigger and then, just then, some more sweat dropped into my eye and she began to stand up and I blowed her away.

"She tumbled back into the water. Splashed a lot at first but, after a while, she quit. Time came I finished the toke and went on back to camp.

"Just one shot. Ain't that something? Always was good with a rifle. Got a sharpshooter on the M14. But I still think about her some. Like maybe I shouldn't have done it. But I can't see no reason why not.

"Ain't no big thing.

"Another shot?"

After supper, waiting for dark. Short and Ripper were talking. Rose was lifting weights, and I was sitting on my bunk, reading, when Tony broke in on us. Something on his radio.

Ripper and Short and Frank bolted for the boats and the guy from South Carolina shrank into his bunk. I didn't know what was going on, but whatever it was, I was going to be in a boat to see it.

Sergeant Stamford tried to intercept me.

"You sure you want to do this?"

Hell, yes, I wanted to do it. I could see the others already piling on board. I was with them before they got away.

The boat stood up with a roar and rolled us all back toward the frothing yellow water. We stormed upriver. I didn't know why. Maybe we'd been caught in a stampede.

> The Magical Mystery Tour
> Is coming to take you away.
> Coming to take you away.
> Take you today.

Yellow water spewed behind us while Ripoli perched in the bow, waving directions at Short. When he motioned to throttle back, the boat mushed into the water until it was almost level. So soft it felt like we'd stopped.

We crawled in and out along the bank, with Ripoli shouting directions and Frank in the bow, jabbing the boat hook at anything he didn't recognize. He never said what he was looking for.

Pleasant enough. For a while. Until the clean smell of warm water sank beneath foulness like dead squirrels.

Rottenness washed over us until it saturated our thoughts. Anything else—the glare of the sun, the sound of Ripper calling Short, the feel of water splashing our arms—was just so much distraction. Interruptions quickly forgotten.

Ripoli grew more urgent. He'd found something. A dim light flickering a few meters from the bank, surrounded by mud and stink; a small upright rectangle floating on the water. As we got closer it broke into patterns. A delicate tracery. Five vertical lines, splayed slightly at the top. Familiar. Almost religious. A small icon set in a luminous aura.

We were on it before I could make out those elegant lines: the bottom of a foot with the bones exposed. A halo of skin curling to the sides and the ankle thrown over a small log. A filleted foot.

We had been racing toward a corpse, pale green as the bottom of a lake.

> The Magical Mystery Tour
> Is dying to take you away.
> Dying to take you away
> Take you today.

Short pulled us next to it. Frank was ready with the boat hook, but Ripper reached in and grabbed an arm. Then, dead slow so it wouldn't unravel, Short gentled it over to the bank, where Ripper tied it to a bush.

Sometimes the head would loll back and the neck open into a dark purse, layers of cut flesh fluttering like sea creatures. Then the head would roll forward and the throat would close into a half-seen line. Hardly more than an inconvenience.

I didn't look away until Short touched my shoulder.

"Why don't you put some water in the motor?"

I don't know if he meant to do me a favor. I dipped the ammo can over the upstream side. It was good to have something to do. I blessed Short for it.

We couldn't leave until Ripper was done fumbling with the wedding ring. Then Short motioned to cast off and we backed away slowly, taking a few more breaths of poisoned air. Anywhere else Short would have shoved into full reverse and we would have shot back like there were snipers. Finally we were clear and heading down the river like we had never been there at all.

A murdered village chief. You could tell by the throat. As stylized as a Mafia killing.

Friendly village chiefs had their throats cut in the thousands. Messy. And they were dumped into the rivers in the hundreds. Cleaned them up some, but also brought terrible effort and sorrow to relatives who couldn't swim.

We'd tied him to the bank for the sake of his family. A martial courtesy, comrade to comrade, if we'd chosen the right bank. I never learned who they thought took the ring.

Something else. You never adjust to some smells. Not like you've been told. When we were back at the bridge the wind blew the stink of that murdered ally over us. It lingered after the body had been taken from the river, and we could not clean ourselves in there again. Even today, so many years away, the smell chokes me.

■ FLARES

THE WATCHES OF THE NIGHT

Flares dropped out of gunships all night, burning the eyes like flashbulbs. One by one they lit the heavens for a moment, blazed, and went out. But none ever burned out before another had taken its place. And no used canisters ever tumbled onto the land. Too hot. Too dangerous. The air crews were too good for that. Spent flares sizzled into the water. No danger out there. Not to anybody but me. They hadn't expected anybody on the river.

HISSSSSSSSSSSSSSSSSSSSSSSSSSSSSSSSSSSSSSSSSSSSSSSSSSSSSSSS

I dodged them by luck. When they were lit and easy to see, they were a focus of attention. But when their fires went out, it was all guess as to where they would whirl on their parachutes, drifting silent as vampires, looking for a shoulder to light on.

The generator had burned out just before dark—I wondered if someone had forgotten to put water in it—and all the lights were out. Nobody had wanted to bring a generator out at night, so they convoyed light to us instead. A plane would spiral around and around, spitting flares, until its replacement slid in behind. Precision and care. We didn't see much of that side of the war.

SSSSSSSSSHHHHHHHHHHHHHHHHHHHHHHHHHHHHP

During the day the bridge was as solid and as utilitarian as an army truck. At night it was delicately lit, when the generator was working, by a lace of bulbs that played over textured sandbags, soaring steel, and rough concrete. A tracery of light that spilled onto the river, browning the watery shadows. From a distance it looked homey. Like a firelit cabin seen from some wild place.

The flares, too, were beautiful. Like golden sparks drifting down at a Fourth of July celebration. Only the light they brought with them was ugly. Bright and flat and the colors weren't right. The strident light that shines in prison yards; the anticrime lights in parking lots. Ugly and filled with foreboding. It gathered where it fell, and it did not warm nearby places. Beneath that light the bridge stood abstract like a cardboard backdrop, the men underneath it lost in shadow.

Each flare whirled down, swinging blackness across the face of the bridge and billowing shadows like ink over the river. The bridge dipped and jerked like a moth flicking around a candle. Then another flare would blaze, and for a while, two sets of shadows would come together like the wings of a fly until the lower light tapered out and the upper was left swinging alone over a new landscape. And then a newer flare would blaze.

HISSSSSSSSSSSSSSSSSSSSSSSSSSSsssssssssssssssssshhhhhhhhhhhhp

But for all their intensity and their ugliness, they did the job. They lit the area and reminded a watching enemy that we were ready.

Nobody attacked us that night. But then, nobody was ready to attack. We were the only ones with contingency plans for burnt-out generators.

■ SHOOTING BUSHES

It had the irregular rhythm of a string of giant firecrackers: sharp and concussive and then the quick sequence of timed bursts. It woke me in the middle of the day.

Firing all along the bridge. Out of bunkers lined up like gun ports on sailing ships. From soldiers arrayed over the rail like executioners. Machine guns. M16s. Rifle grenades. Continuous fire in just the time it took to slap in a new belt or magazine. All of it to keep a dark object from drifting onto the log boom.

We fired at it because we didn't know what it was. But for all our fury it kept coming, shrouded behind a curtain of white spray.

The time had passed when I could take out a squad of infantry onto the wild river and look at it. We had to wait for it to come to us. And we kept firing. Thousands, maybe tens of thousands, of dollars worth of ordnance.

Steel and spray. And it kept coming.

Maybe we should have used silver bullets.

At last it drifted up to the log boom. And halted there. We stopped firing long enough for Frank to go out and check it.

Bushes. A big clump of bushes. Fallen into the river downstream and washed up to the bridge.

Just bushes.

All that steel. All those throbbing bullets and scraps of razor-sharp wire. Everywhere little pieces of bush had danced off. The mass had trembled and jumped. But when it was over, when our weapons were stilled, nothing had changed. It had drifted up to our log boom just as it had set out to do. So much power and we could not deflect it.

■ POLICING THE BATTLEFIELD

S ergeant Stamford had us in an empty field in wolfhound territory. A back slope between the bunkers and the wire. A place we had never seen. A place for us to clean.

It already looked clean to me. We must have done something wrong.

And now, direct from the world, the ARMED FORCES RADIO AND TELEVISION NETWORK PRESENTS THIS WEEK'S *NEWS AND ANALYSIS*.

American runners Tommie Smith and John Carlos placed first and third in the two-hundred-meter dash. But as the band struck up "The Star Spangled Banner" for the awards ceremony, the two black athletes bowed their heads and raised clenched fists in black gloves. Black power salutes. Setting off one of the most unpleasant controversies in Olympic history.

Not much to pick up out there. Just scraps. A few butts and little pieces of foil. Pop tops. None of the big stuff. No cans. No soggy newspapers. Hardly seemed worth it.

In other Olympic news, Bob Beamons of the University of Texas set a new world record in the long jump, shattering the old mark by almost . . .

We headed down the hill side by side in a line which bent whenever one of us squatted to reach into the grass. Awkward like a harvesting machine that's been left too long in the rain.

America kept the bands working as Al Oerter claimed the discus laurels with a throw of 212 feet 6½ inches. . . .

When we got near the wire, I hung back. I didn't want to find any trash in there.

. . . in Skorpios. The adverse reaction to Mrs. Kennedy's marriage flows straight from the expectations of her countrymen. The beautiful princess had run off with a toad. And worse, her marriage symbolized the end of an era. The end of Camelot. A time when Americans felt better about being Americans.

We hovered in the shadow of the wire until Sergeant Stamford looked the other way. Then we turned and headed back up the hill with our little balls of wrappers and cigarette papers. I wondered where they'd come from. Who would stroll in such a place?

Smith and Carlos stepped down to a chorus of boos, and they replied to their Mexican hosts with more salutes. Single-fingered salutes in black gloves.

I left a pink wad of gum stuck to the leg of a claymore. It was biodegradable. And so was I.

Later Carlos explained what they meant to accomplish.
"White people think we're animals. I want them to know we're not animals, not inferior animals like cats and rats. They think we're some sort of show horse. They think we will perform and they will throw in some peanuts and say 'good boy. Good boy. . . .'"

We walked back, kicking for the small stuff. Picking through patches of grass like birds on a rhino.

Bob Beamons may be the most unlikely jumper in world class competition. Sometimes he doesn't bother to count his strides on the approach and he takes off from either foot. He is awkward in the air, his body jackknifes, and his legs are spread-eagled long before he dumps into the pit. But when they taped off his heel print, he had sailed 29 feet 2½ inches. Almost 2 feet more than the previous world record. The men who held that record were sitting on the bench while he did it.

We dribbled our wet loads into a black plastic bag and wiped our hands on our pants. Then we filed around to the side of the field to glean trash at right angles.

. . . Al Oerter has never been favored to win the event he does so well, but in 1956 he beat Fortune Gordien to take the gold in Melbourne. In 1960, in Rome, he won over another teammate, Rink Babka, and in Tokyo in 1964 he beat Czechoslovakia's Ludvik Danek.

Cleaning an abandoned field. Such a forlorn extravagance.
"Who we cleaning this place for, Sarge?"
"Yeah, Charlie's gonna be coming through there some day. Without us to clean the way, maybe he'll cut himself on a tab and get infected off one of them nasty damn butts and have to get medevaced back to fucking Hanoi for some fucking hospital time."

. . . a match not approved by the Kennedys, with whom she was never close.

"Geneva convention, Troop. No biologicals. No infections. Have to keep Charlie clean."
"Well, what's the shit he smears on his pungi sticks? Penicillin?"
"Charlie didn't sign no Geneva Convention."

The theological complications of the union are even more convoluted than the social. As a Roman Catholic, Mrs. Kennedy cannot marry a divorced man. Under the Greek Orthodox creed, Onassis may marry three, not four but three, times. After this wedding he is expected to seek an annulment of his previous marriage. When it is granted the new Mrs. Onassis will petition the Vatican to pass on the validity of her new marriage. This reporter has been unable to determine whether the annulment, if granted, will make the Onassis children illegitimate. Perhaps Thomas Aquinas would know.

"Charlie can do any DAMN thing he pleases. We got to follow the Geneva MOTHER FUCKING Convention. What kind of shit is that?"
"Our shit."

Angry and humiliated, the U.S. Olympic Committee strongly reprimanded Smith and Carlos and formally apologized to the International Olympic Committee, the Mexican Organizing Committee, and the Mexican people.

It took a lot of pointing and naming names, but eventually Sergeant Stamford got us lined up. When he estimated we were as orderly as he could make us, he sent us back across the field, staring at the ground like condemned men.

    . . . not enough for eighty-one-year-old Avery Brundage, who threatened to expel the entire American team unless Smith and Carlos were actually punished. The U.S. Olympic Committee promptly suspended the two and evicted them from the American quarters.

You cross a field a different way, and you see different things. The first pass left that hill as spotless as the yard around a funeral home. But when we went back over it crosswise, wet cigarette butts bloated under our feet like maggots waiting to grow into tropical flies.

In 1935 Jesse Owen set a long jump record of 26 feet $8\frac{1}{4}$ inches that stood for a quarter century. Since 1960, America's Ralph Boston and Russia's Igor Ter-Ovanesyan have repeatedly broken that record, trading the title back and forth. As the nineteenth games opened, they were coholders of the record at 27 feet $4\frac{3}{4}$ inches, a full $8\frac{1}{2}$ inches over Jesse Owen's mark.

When we got to the far edge, we turned and wandered back across the field, carrying our squashy loads, warm tobacco juice running down our wrists and gum wrappers sparkling between our fingers. Sergeant Stamford waited contentedly by the radio, holding the plastic bag.

Garlanded with lemon buds flown in from Holland, the wedding party boarded their white honeymoon yacht to dine on exotic dainties and rare wines brought by waiting lighters.

We may have been done picking up the trash, but we sure weren't done talking about it.

"Look here, Sarge. Nothing's ever happened here. No outdoor music festivals. No firefights. Nothing. Time to clean a place is AFTER something's happened."

"You want to clean up after a firefight? That it? You ever been around after a firefight? All you've ever been is in the motor pool and down by the river where it's all perfumed and sunny. You see a battlefield AFTER a firefight someday, it's got a different kind of perfume. Little pieces of things. Unexploded ordnance and the ground isn't near so even as before.

> . . . She is reported to have her clothing arranged by primary colors and shades. Closets for day suits and closets for evening suits, evening dresses arranged by length, and hundreds of shoes cataloged by color and style. It's not known how much of this the new Mrs. Onassis will take to Skorpios and how much she will just buy again when she gets there. . . .

"You stick around. You'll get your chance. Some morning there'll be a firefight right over there. Lots of scraps when it's done. Charlie all mingled up with your buddies. Then you can go tiptoeing through, filling bags. Sometimes you won't need more than a sandwich bag, others you'll need a double-strength Hefty bag. No end to the bags you're gonna need.

> In 1963 Oerter slipped a cervical disk and has competed in a surgical collar ever since. He takes it off only for the Olympics. "These are the Olympics—you die for them."

"Toss it all in—heads, feet, knees, asses, shoulders, elbows, toenails. Keep at it until you've got you a person in there.

> In Tokyo he beat Czechoslovakia's favorite, Ludwig Danek, while hemorrhaging from a torn leg cartilage. This week he upset Jay Silvester, another favored teammate, while staggering from a torn thigh muscle.

"Nothing's official until you toss in the dog tags. So pick them up first. Otherwise somebody else'll get them, and you gonna have all those bags you can't do anything with. And make sure the dog tags match. Else you're gonna get a visit from a lieutenant inquiring as to precedence.

> When he set the Olympic shotput mark, he set another record as well, becoming the only competitor in Olympic history to win the same event four times.

"I used to put in a few extra parts sometimes. Sarge'd say, 'You got you a person in there, Son?' I'd say, 'A person, Sarge? I got me BETTER than a person in here.'

■
Phu
Cuong

He was already looking toward Munich and his fifth gold when we asked about his phenomenal ability to overcome age and physical handicap. "I think I can continue to improve until forty or so. . . . "

"Don't overdo it, though. Folks back home don't want to be burying any wrong people. And they know, too. They weigh them. One time we sent home about 220 pounds of Martin. All those Martins back in Cedar Rapids, they knew their boy didn't weigh more than 150. Tried to send him back to us, too, but the APO wouldn't have it.

Ter-Ovanesyan spoke for everyone who saw Beamons jump. "Compared to that, the rest of us are children."

"Truth was, I'd sent them about as much of Martin as I could lay my hands on. Just wasn't all Martin. I'd fleshed him out with other parts. Didn't want anybody feeling short-ordered.

. . . Beamons sank to his knees in the pit. "I was thanking that man up there for letting me hit the ground right here."

"Can't get everything into the bags. What you really want to do is hose the place off. But it doesn't help much. Takes flies to clean a place right."

This reporter noted that, when "The Star Spangled Banner" was played for Smith and Carlos, athletes from every other nation present—Soviet and East German and even Cuban— stood at rigid attention.

■ COMPACT

A clipping from the *Atlanta Constitution*. Tuesday, September 25, 1968. Page 17.

Jerry Sand was back in the news. My childhood buddy had a talent for publicity. In April he had been news in every paper in the patriotic South.

ATLANTA SOLDIER DESERTS.

Off to Sweden when he was supposed to be in Vietnam. And he was only a clerk. Meant to type in a base camp. To give himself promotions and to take R and R's.

I thought he'd overreacted.

We'd all pictured him eating lunch in the arctic shadows, the sun setting beneath his feet. Trudging through dark snow, looking for work. Grappling with Swedish.

Other people thought about him, too. A disc jockey lobbied to be sent to Sweden for a "historical interview with Atlanta's only deserter." He got a transatlantic phone call and the opportunity to swap wisdom at twenty-three dollars a minute. No surprises. Until he asked Jerry whether he'd seen his clippings. Jerry had. He didn't like them. Didn't think he was getting favorable coverage.

"Well, what the hell did you expect, friend, a medal of honor?"

The DJ was a fleeting hero for that. Hundreds of calls to the station. Most thought he should have used stronger language. Some were so explicit the station reported them to the Georgia Bureau of Investigation.

Angry people. A mob at the airport, waiting for Jerry to come back.

All but me. I didn't care where Jerry was, just where I'd be. In a few months I'd be home. An American. It was my compact with the United States. It was a good reason to go to Vietnam.

In a year Jerry would still be in the dark snow. And in five years he'd be there. And in ten.

He would see his parents only when they came to him, and he would never show his children the places of his own childhood. His wife would be foreign and his children would be foreign and they would speak a language he would never master and he would not be there to comfort his mother when his father died. And as he got older, he would think more about where he had come from and what he was doing so far from his own people.

Phu
Cuong

> Georgia, Georgia,
> No peace I find,
> Just an old sweet song keeps
> Georgia on my mind.

And that, too, was my compact with the United States.

■ DRAWING BLOOD

THE WATCHES OF THE NIGHT

Grenades rolled off the bridge in a slow cascade. Sometimes one landed close enough to rock the boat and shoot acid through our nerves.

Fucked-up Arvins.

I wondered if Short were going to make an example of somebody.

He didn't have to.

"OH, SHIT."

Three figures plunged out of a bunker. The pier in front of us flashed black while the concrete facing the bunker glared a hateful gray-white. A fragmentation grenade bursting in air. A hard noise slapped our ears.

Short was out of the boat and toward those people before the sound had reached the far bank.

He came back with one of the wolfhounds. Dragging an Arvin. They had their arms around his and his head rolled forward, his knees bent and his toes scraping. I couldn't see him well, in and out of the shadows, but I couldn't make out anything wrong, either. No marks. No blood. Maybe he was drunk.

They lowered him to the deck face down, as if he'd drowned, and I saw his back. Full of hot steel wires. He'd been running like the others.

I rode up front with him while the boat slammed toward the chopper pad. His trouser leg had been blown off, and his calf was mostly gone. Torn like crabs had been at it. Blood welled all over his leg. A hundred wounds too deep to staunch.

Holes burned in his uniform at his neck and his shoulders, his arms, his spine and his kidneys, his buttocks, his genitals, and all over his legs. Blood bubbled from every hole and spread over his back in dark circles. Too many.

He squirmed a little and opened and closed his hand on the deck.
214 He might have been trying to tell me something. I couldn't tell.

> Oh yeah, I'll tell you something
> I think you'll understand,
> Then I'll say that something
> I want to hold your hand,
> I want to hold your hand,
> I want to hold your hand.

I hesitated, and then we were on the other bank and he was unloaded. I lost the chance.

I wish I had him back now.

> And please say to me
> You'll let me hold your hand.

After he was gone, I rinsed the deck with river water. It didn't take so much.

I went back to his bunker. It was a mess. Piss and dried puke. A small wooden table blown over and as full of holes as a rural stop sign. The sandbags were all leaking. Liquor and glass were puddled on the floor. An Arvin was shrieking at a wolfhound, and they were both screaming at another wolfhound. The one who'd dropped the grenade. An American had dropped it on an Arvin. After all those nights on the river, it was us who hurt them.

"Dead. Died twice on the pad, and they brought him around. Then he died again."

Ripoli climbed into the bunker.

"It was bright where they laid him. They cut off his clothes and you could see his back good. You should have stuck around."

After a while people starting playing cards and dropping grenades in the river and smoking again. The bottles and the baggies came out and things got back to normal. The odd thing was that nobody ever seemed to notice what had happened. No officer came. No sergeant took charge, and as far as I know, none ever thought he should have.

Ripper took Short back to shore. It was my night to be on the river.

The wolfhound was still in a fog. I guess I would have been, too. He kept holding his right hand—his grenade hand—in front of him, making squeezing motions. Then he turned his arm over and a dark trace of blood ran down his wrist.

"Look at that, you've been hit."

He hadn't noticed before.

"Ain't that some shit? Think I'll get a purple heart?"

What a thing to ask. But I guess he needed something to think about. And medication. Just like that Arvin he'd killed.

He kept opening and closing the hand, squeezing blood into his palm. And he needed more than medication. He needed comforting.

> Yeah, you got that something
> I think you'll understand
> When I say that something
> I want to hold your hand.

■ BOB HOPE

When Bob Hope stepped onstage, we threw beer cans at him. Some of those cans still held beer and cartwheeled forward in spirals of white foam. His cameramen hunched down on their little platforms, looking small before the sudden storm.

The date for the show had been secret, but we had known for some time he was on his way. As it turned out, the secret wasn't any better kept than most of our other secrets. The day he arrived, we knew before reveille. All the nonessential personnel—that is to say, almost everyone at Cu Chi and a lot of us from the field—got the day off. We bought as much beer as we could carry and made it over to the field where the show was scheduled. Hundreds, maybe thousands, of us were there by nine. A steady stream drifted in throughout the long day. But we got there first, and we had the best place: right in front of the stage, slightly up the hill.

It started as a picnic spread over hard dirt. Beer in the morning. No details. No patrols. Just drink and brag in the sun. A perfect day, lying on a blanket.

But the perfect day wore on too long. The tropic sun hung overhead, with beer the only treatment for it. That endless hot morning was punctuated only by trips to the PX and visits to the latrine. The beer in the sun got warm, and the new beer was already warm. The PX couldn't chill it fast enough.

Soldiers kept streaming in until, by early afternoon, the place was running out of room. People who had spread out on the dirt all morning had to pull in their legs and then their arms. Later we sat up.

Late arrivals hadn't seen a beer since the night before, and those just back from patrol had gone dry a lot longer. It was a holiday, and they were ready to party. But their timing wasn't ours. We had been sucking brew since before breakfast. We were sleepy. We had headaches. The sun hurt our eyes, and the PX was out of aspirin. We didn't want to be jostled, and we didn't want to listen to radios or hear war stories. We just wanted to lie down, but there wasn't any place.

All around was shoving and threats, but there wasn't any trou- 217 ble. The show was scheduled for 15:00, and that was soon enough. We just kept sliding over and scrunching up and trying to keep from puking on each other. Finally, a colonel stepped out and signaled for quiet. He got it. Things were beginning to happen, but when he talked, only the people in the very front could hear.

"What did he say?"

"I couldn't hear. HEY. WHAT DID HE SAY?"

"Beats shit out of me."

Ripples surged through the crowd, fanning out from the colonel. They reached the people in front of me, and then I knew.

"Fucking A, man, how late?"

"How the shit should I know?"

"Raggedy-assed fucking way to run a war, if you ask me."

"AH, FUCK, man. I sit here all FUCKING day, and I gotta be out on the FUCKING line at 18:00. MOTHER FUCK. We oughta just split. You know what I mean?"

We knew just what he meant. The only reason we didn't split was because we had such good seats. Best seats in the place. We'd sat there all day to hold them. If we had to, we'd sit there another day to keep them. It seemed like we did.

Fifteen hundred hours came and went. No Bob Hope and no word why. Or when. We kept sitting and drinking and picking our way out of the crowd to stand in the latrine.

About suppertime the ripples told us that Bob Hope's plane had landed.

Half an hour later his people showed up—civilians to lay out speakers and set up lights. It wasn't the show, but it was something to watch. And that crew was pretty good, with all their moving and switching. A sort of preliminary show before the main attraction. It was worth seeing.

I was so taken with it that I didn't see the second crew until it shoved us aside to lay plywood panels on the ground. Before the show started, those panels became the biggest, ugliest, and opaquist camera platform I have ever seen. Men in earphones rolled back and forth on cameras in front of our show while we shoved around on the dirt, making helpless comments.

"Who's this fuckin show FOR, dude?"

"MISTER Hope come all the way to the Nam to take mother fucking home movies of hisself?"

"SHEE-IT. We be sending those mofo cameras and those mon-key-assed earphones on a tour of they own without Mr. Hope."

"You want to go along, MISTER cameraman? You can hump that mother FUCKIN' camera up to the Cambodian border. Get some real pictures of this mother fuckin' place."

It may have been the earphones, or maybe they had gone through this before, but they didn't seem to notice.

An hour earlier, before we knew Bob Hope had landed, it would have been a riot. Those cameras would have been cremated on a pyre of burning plywood. As it was, we just moved off to the side, sitting with our knees pulled to our chests among strangers not glad to have us.

Headaches cut our peripheral vision to what we could have seen through a keyhole, and we were throbbing with the need to piss, but nobody wanted to give up his little place in the dirt, so nobody went. We just waited, thousands of legs clamped against the pressure and thousands of brains strobing in pain.

Most of us had left our inhibitions out in the field somewhere and had brought back a hot sun of frustration burning in our chests. Sitting in the dirt, drinking beer, we had had a long hot day to study the frustrations of our lives. By the time we had finally discovered that Bob Hope stood at their very center, there he was—strolling on stage, swinging a golf club. We needed more transition.

He was almost center stage before somebody threw the first can. And the fires in our chests leaped and danced at the sight of it, arching over the crowd. We all found eight-ounce missiles in our hands where beer cans had been. We all stood and threw. If we had any other cans, we threw them as well. Given the state of our bladders, I do not believe all of those cans held beer.

The intent to throw had never been in us. It came from our eyes and ran straight to our arms and did not involve our thoughts. It happened the way the first clap sets loose a roomful of applause: after it is ended, you can find no one who thought to clap.

Bob Hope handled it well. He swung at the first can with his golf club while his little band made swinging noises. Then he must have seen light flash from another can somewhere out front because he looked up into a frothy wave about to crest over his head.

When the cans finally stopped dancing and rolling, the fires in our chests had burned down to coals and we all sat down and laughed.

The colonel kicked his way back onto the stage, and this time we could all hear him. There weren't going to be any more insults to our guest. And he was right. By then we didn't have any reason to throw things, and we wanted to hang onto our beer.

They shoveled off the stage and mopped it. Bob Hope adlibbed his way back on, with a helmet and a whole bag full of clubs. Said he thought he might need them.

Once, when I was in college, I'd seen another Bob Hope show. It wasn't the same. This was the real thing, fleshed out of what the college show could only hint at: genuinely undressed ladies doing seriously dirty things. Ten thousand Nikons and Pentaxes filled with images of sweet, fluffy snatch and pink nipples and heavy, succulent tits dripping out of sequinned gowns. It was a show to make the Romans blush, and it was a show worth seeing. It really did what Bob Hope always said it did: it took the boys' minds off the war.

Thanks for the mammaries.

■ DREAMS

I made her beg.

"Please," she begged, when she saw me in the doorway.

But "please" wasn't enough. Not nearly enough.

Hope Cook swayed her hips as she shrugged out of the top of her robe, filling the room with bobbing tits and tight nipples. "Please. Don't make me do it again."

But it's what she wanted, too. She pulled back the sash and the robe piled around her feet. She waited naked for me to see. She already had her hand between her legs.

"Please don't."

She began moving her hips. And rubbing her thighs. And pulling her breasts. I could smell her fishy perfume across the room. And she knew it.

She came toward me, trembling. Hardly able to walk. When she was close enough she reached for my crotch. She'd wanted to wrap her lips around me ever since she'd seen me in the caravan.

"Please. Now. Please. I . . . "

She settled softly to her knees, fumbling with my zipper. Then she groped inside. She shivered when she felt the throbbing in her hand.

"Please. I need. . . . "

She rubbed it back and forth along her cheek until I was dancing in place with her head. Then she moaned and slipped her mouth over it.

I tangled her hair and held on, pumping like a steam engine, while her free hand moved over her body, tugging and rubbing and squeezing. Her body stiffened as I anointed the back of her throat. She grabbed her cunt and gave a strangled shout that should have roused the king in the next bed.

The thing about jerking off is that you don't have to get dressed up for it. And you don't have to worry about the Chinese clap and evil women waiting to surprise you with razor blades inside.

Freckled Hope Cook was the sexiest woman in the world, to me. I'd taped her picture over my bunk, but nobody else under the bridge seemed to like her at all. As far as I could tell, only one other man in the world had even noticed her. The king of Sikkim.

Trouble was, my beautiful Hope Cook was up in Sikkim, sleeping with him, right then. If only she'd known about me.

The picture was entitled "America's only queen." After all, Grace was just a princess.

The picture didn't mention it, but she was also Sikkim's only queen.

The other thing about jerking off is that it's messy. Instead of being absorbed in Hope Cook's eager face, my progeny lay wriggling on the mattress like a cold puddle of Elmer's Glue. Millions and millions of little half me's swimming on identical frantic missions that would never be fulfilled alone in a bed. Or in anybody's mouth.

So much life cooling on that mattress. Soon there would be more deaths there than in the whole of the war. Probably than in all the wars. So much potential. Individuals to save the world. If only I could pick them out, somehow, and slip them up Loi, or one of those women back under the low part of the bridge, the war— everything—would be worthwhile.

Somewhere else in that squirming puddle were the genes to end it all. Evil to swallow Hitler or Ho Chi Minh. I would pluck it out and stomp it into the dirt, if I could. A batch of sperm for women to step lightly around.

But most of them would be just people. Saints of the ordinary.

> And one was a doctor, and one was a queen,
> And one was a shepherdess on the green. . . .

Scores of millions of men and women just to go to work every day and home every night and into the army when they were called. People to hold the world together for all those who have more important things to do.

> And one was a soldier, and one was a priest,
> And one was slain by a fierce wild beast.

And one for a miner, and one to pour steel, and one to be blind and move by feel. And one for a cold death of cold, and one to feel heat, and one to grow food for the rest to eat.

■ DAY ON THE DOCK

Election Day: Tuesday, 5 Nov '68. 09:00. The prettiest day I spent at the bridge. Also the last.

I'd been on patrol the night before, and it was my turn to sleep. But it was too pretty to be indoors. So I grabbed my copy of *Lady Chatterley's Lover,* as many C's as my stomach could tolerate, and headed for the dock. The yellow tide was two-thirds in and rising.

As I napped, the river rose. In what seemed a matter of seconds—like watching time-lapse movies of plants wave about and die—the boats were green walls bobbing around my head. The river was nearly still. I sat up and dangled my feet over the side.

Altogether the prettiest day I was in Vietnam.

> Sittin' in the morning sun.
> I'll be sitting when the evenin' come.
> Watchin' the ships roll in,
> Then watch 'em roll away again.

Fresh and bright. Even for Charlie. No signs of war. No choppers, no distant bombing, no mortars, no rockets. Like being up at Lake Lanier with a magazine on your face.

I lay back down and watched the river through the places between the boards. When my back got hot, I'd roll over and when my chest got hot, I'd drop into the yellow water. The fall was farther each time, and the climb out was longer. The water was always just as black when it closed over my head, but it washed off the heat.

There were suds back under the bridge. When the day got hot enough I went for some. Everybody was asleep. Beer without disputes.

Drinking beer alone in the sun, you think things you wouldn't think otherwise. I thought about how not a single grenade had dropped into my boat the night before. So much fear and no letdown when it ended. But there was always the next night.

And I thought about my friends who would never come to Vietnam. I thought how long it would take to get back to them in my

223

fast boat. And how far it was by airplane. And who knew who'd be glad to see me. And whether I should feel let down by them instead.

> Sittin' here restin' my bones,
> And this loneliness won't leave me alone.
> Two thousand miles I roam
> Just to make this dock my home.

■ SWAPPING SCRIP

The Oriental Bazaar and International Currency Exchange
was open for business. Right under the bridge.
"Fitysen-dollah."
Orange paper tangled in dirty fists.
"Numbah one deal, yes?"
A very good price to hold paper for an hour. But
"How did they know? Nobody told *us* about any swap."
"Never say. Just say 'fitysen-dollar.'"
Little Brown Brother, tied to the American economy. Swapping
his work and his goods for orange American cash.

LEGAL TENDER FOR ALL DEBTS PUBLIC AND PRIVATE.

Redeemable at any American installation.
But only by us. All the rest was black market money.

LEGAL TENDER FOR ALL STREET DEBTS AND SECRET
DEALINGS.

And when there was too much of that, our government repudi-
ated the entire run and issued a new batch in a different color. It
never announced a swap. It just sent officers by with boxes of the
new money.

And every time, just hours before it did, Vietnamese swarmed
like insurance salesmen.

"You give money, lieutenant. Keep half. Fitysen-dollah. Numbah
one deal."

It cut the cost of the war. Every dollar that got lost was a dollar
the government never had to honor. Hundreds of millions of them.
Savings courtesy of the Vietnamese entrepreneur. The capitalists
we had come to save.

Long before the officers arrived, we all had pockets full of orange
paper.

"Count too many of those things, Tony, the ink'll come off on
your fingers and they'll treat you for jaundice."   225

"I get that many and they can treat me for gone. Then little Brown Brother can give you the jaundice."

"Strange, isn't it?"

"What?"

"How they know about the swaps."

"Just know, I guess."

"But how? That's what I want to find out."

"Friends tell them."

"But somebody had to know first. And he didn't have any way to find out, Tony. No PHYSICAL way. Army sure didn't tell him. Only one way he could have known."

Tony sat up.

"Courses, Tony. Some English-speaking son of a bitch out there sent off for one of your courses. They're studying to be Rosicrucians. Rosi-fucking-crucians."

"What? You sure?"

That was the great thing about Tony. There were no limits to what he would believe. He was a fountain of entertainment. Lately I have grown to have more respect for a gentle heart and less for a quick mind, but at the time I enjoyed our relationship.

"Of course, I'm sure. Just ask one."

"YOU. Yeah, you. How you know about swap?"

"Know? Just know."

"Okay, just know. HOW you just know?"

"Just know, Joe. Just know. You want money. Only fitysen-dollah? Number one deal."

"No want money. You Rosicrucian? You study Rosicrucian? You tell me. You Rosicrucian?"

He didn't answer, just backed away, smiling and nodding. Thought he would take his trade to the wolfhounds. Tony just saw the smiling and the nodding.

"I told you they're taking the courses. You've got to let somebody know. This is serious."

"Me?"

"Sure you. What do I know about Rosicrucians? You're the only one can do that propeller stuff. You've got to make them believe, Tony. Before it's too late."

"Who . . . ?"

"Tell Stamford. Better yet, tell one of the officers when they come by with the new scrip. This is big. You bick?"

"I may not be here then."

"You're always here."

"Not tonight. Tonight they want me over to Bien-Cat. Didn't say why. Hope everybody's okay over there. You tell the officers."

That conversation had sure taken a nasty turn.

Little Brown Brother was still streaming in.

"You give me back all dollah. I give you Seiko."

A new wrinkle.

> I'll give you a diamond ring, my friend,
> If it makes you feel all right
> I'll get you anything my friend,
> If it makes you feel all right
> For I don't care too much for money,
> Money can't buy me love.

Ripoli took the orange bills. He always did like jewelry. Little Brown Brother hung onto the Seiko. It glinted on his wrist.

"Twenty-fivesen-dollah. Twenty-fivesen-dollah."

Time must be running out.

"I can't take that. Who's ever gonna believe I carry ten thousand dollars in cash? I only draw fifty dollars a month. No can do."

"Yes, can do. Pokah. You play pokah. Tell lieutenant you play pokah."

"How you gonna get your money when I'm in the Long Binh jail?"

"Long Binh very good. Have cousin in Long Binh. He bring you money. You see."

"I can't take it all."

"Just these. I write how much. Receipt you. Receipt me. You bick?"

I bicked.

> I'll give you all I have to give
> If you say you love me, too.
> I may not have a lot to give,
> What I've got I'll give to you,
> For I don't care too much for money,
> For money can't buy me love.

Crafty Brown Brother evaporated into the sun, replaced by American officers and a square metal box. One by one, we counted orange cash onto a footlocker. An officer laid out blue cash next to it.

"You got seventeen years' pay there, soldier."

"Poker, sir."

"Well, you're mighty God damn good at it, aren't you? Everybody out here seems to be mighty God damn good at cards. Win all this money from each other?"

"We're a lucky outfit, sir."

"I can see that. With that kind of God damn luck, you should be at the Pentagon, running the God damn war."

"I've often had that thought myself, sir."

"Well, take your God damn pile of money, soldier, and don't go giving it to any God damn Gooks. That's God damn American money there. You understand?"

"Yes, sir."

They took their gray box and moved on. I was still sitting next to Tony.

"Tell them about the Rosicrucians?"

"Hell, no. Those guys don't know from spiritual."

"Been thinking about that."

"About what?"

"Spiritual. You know what day it is, Tony?"

"Big deal. I can't even vote."

"No. Not Election Day."

"It is Election Day."

"Your dream, Tony. This is the day Charlie hits the bridge. You seen any Charlies?"

"You never see any Charlies."

"Yeah, but today? You ever see a place so peaceful? Could be Easter back home. Even the spotters in the sampans have taken the day off."

He surprised me with how dignified he got.

"Look, I never said Charlie'd hit the bridge. I just told you what the dream said, okay?"

"So what did the dream say about me? Was I hit?"

"I don't know. I didn't see you."

"Well, what did it say about you, then? You must have seen yourself."

"It said I wasn't going to be here."

"But you're always here."

"Not tonight. Tonight I'm at Bien-Cat."

When little Brown Brother came back, we counted blue notes onto footlockers. There was a little snarling when Ripoli held out for a genuine Seiko.

"Listen, you slope-headed bastard, I don't care how you repainted the son of a bitch. I already got a Timex. Bick?"

Ripper eased over toward the big wrench on the sandbags. But he didn't need it. He held all the money, and that was enough. Little Brown Brother gave it up for lost and jabbered at a kid who handed him something shiny. Ripper took his time examining it, the sun glinting from his teeth. When the money was counted, the man and the boy vanished like leprechauns. They didn't want any reconsideration.

That left Ripoli next to the sandbags, swinging the wrench.

"Any of you ever pick this thing up? I always sort of thought I could do some damage with it. Bash some heads. Now I think maybe I'll use my boot."

He gave it to Tubb.

"Shee-it."

Who passed it to Tony.

"You guys use it. I won't be here."

Who gave it to me.

No substance. A stage-set tool. As light as the batons that relay runners carry. When I tossed it to Rose, it drifted through the air with the grace of a cereal puff in a TV commercial. Magnesium. Another charm against fear.

And one last Brown Brother, come to try his hand.

"TENSEN-dollah. You give tensen blue, I give one dollah orange. Number one deal."

Apparently not everybody was hooked into the Rosicrucians.

Tensen-dollah. Best deal of the day. And none of us wanted it. Nobody except Tony, who bought some on the speculation that orange scrip might come back sometime. Or maybe he wanted souvenirs or just wanted to give the poor guy a break. I never asked.

> Say you don't need no diamond ring,
> And I'll be satisfied.
> Tell me you want those kind of things
> That money just can't buy,
> For I don't care too much for money,
> For money can't buy me love.

■ EXPLOSION

THE WATCHES OF THE NIGHT

There's a place in *Lady Chatterley's Lover* where she decides, in honor of her gamekeeper, to stop wearing underwear. That's as far as I ever got.

A full moon when the sun set and it was Short's last night for guard duty. Also his last night in the country. He began celebrating early. Come dark, we judged he was in no condition to be around boats. Or around weapons. So I took his turn. I wished I could have taken his turn on the plane home.

Nothing more to do out on the water than there ever had been. I tied up to number two pier and settled down to read. The quietest place on the river since Short had introduced himself to the people overhead.

Warm rocking waves lapping against the boat. I idled my way through the life of an English lady and her social climbing employee until she began forming resolutions about her underwear. Then

splsssshh . . . splsssshh . . . B-LAAM . . . splsssshh . . .
BLAM . . . B-LAM . . . splsssshhsplsssshh . . .
B-LAM BLAM . . . splsssshh splsssshh splsssshh
B-LAA-B-LAAM-B-LAAM splsssshh BLAAMBLAAM . . .
Tot . . . tot . . Tot . . TotTotTotTotToT splsssshh
splsssshh . . . Tot Tot BLAAM Tot BLAAM Tot Tot

"What the . . .

Tot tot tot BLAAM . . . splsssshh . . . splsssshh . . .
tot-tot-tot-totBLAAM . . . B-BLAAM . . . tot . . . tot . . .
tot . . . splsssshhsplsssshhsplsssshh . . . tot . . . tot . . .
BLAAB-LAAM . . . tot . . . tot . . . splsssshh . . .
splsssshh . . . splsssshh . . . splsssshh . . . splsssshh . . .
tot . . . tot . . . B-LAMM . . . tot . . . BLAM

230   ". . . HELL are they . . .

PFHUUMP . . . tot . . . tot . . . tot . . . tot . . . tot . . .

plsssshh . . . PFHUUMP . . . tot . . . B-LAAM . . . tot . . .

B-LAAM . . . tot . . . splsssshh . . . tot . . . tot . . . tot . . .

B-LAAM . . . tot . . . tot . . . splsssshh . . . PFHUUMP . . .

B-LAAM . . . tottot . . . splsssshhsplsssshh . . . tot . . .

tot . . . BLABLAAM

". . . doing up there?"

PFHUUMP tot tot tot PFHUUMP splsssshh Bwang tot tot
splsssshh Bang B-wam Tot tot Tot tot tot . . .

Grenades and rifle fire and automatic weapons.

The water boiled with burning steel. A misty wall of frags. A
killing fog. When the noise eased up, the water still steamed and
roiled.

```
tottottot      BLAAM . . . splsssshh . . . tot . . .
PFHUUMP . . . B-LAAM . . . tot . . . tot . . .
splsssshh      B-LAAM      tot  tot  tot  tot
tot            splsssshh                         B-LAAM
                    tottottot           tottot
               splsssshh                         B-LAAM
                    tot      tot
     tot
```

"Get that GOD DAMNED boat out there."

There wasn't much debate as to which boat. So I slipped the
rope, hit the starter, and slid forward.

But why?

"The diver, GOD DAMN IT. The GOD DAMN diver."

"Right on top. Swimming like a son of a bitch. Straight over
there. In the weeds. Get that SON OF A BITCH. MOVE IT."

The rule had always been "Carry your weapon. Wear your
helmet. Wear your flak jacket." And there I was, barefoot, with a
copy of *Lady Chatterley's Lover* and a boat hook clipped to the side
of the passenger compartment. A long wooden pole with a blunt
prod and a short hook. A trainee lance, not meant to hurt anybody.
Still, I sallied into battle with my boat hook ready.

It was prod and jab in the weeds. Move a little. Prod and jab.

That diver couldn't have been very observant. He treated me like I was dangerous. When he got away, I was in no mood to contest his escape.

It didn't occur to me that he knew what he was fleeing and that it wasn't me.

Back at the pier the same voice nagged from above.

"Put on your GOD DAMN life jacket, soldier."

A captain I had once refused to take somewhere until he had put on his own life jacket.

"NOW. GOD DAMN IT."

I was in no position to argue, so I put one on. The only time I ever did.

The grenades came for me again. Dropping like plums after a storm. The people overhead were carpet bombing the river, and they weren't going to miss any part of it, including me.

Clnggggg

Into the boat.

Splsssshh

B-LAAM

And back out.

It couldn't last. The next one that came in would stay in.

I didn't have anywhere to go.

Splsssshh . . . splsssshh . . . B-LAAMsplsssshh
B-LAAAM   splsssshh . . . splsssshh B-LAAM . . . B-LAAM
splsssshh . . .   B-LAAM . . .

T H W O O N M M

Hurtling backward through the air, chin to my chest, arms and legs snapping pinwheels, I never saw the grenade that got me.

What goes up, must come down.
Spinning Wheel got to go 'round.

And into philosophical discourse. Trying to justify myself: "Damn shame. So much I could have done."

> Talkin' 'bout your troubles, it's a cryin' sin,
> Ride a painted pony, let the Spinning Wheel spin.

"So, what have you done already? Quarter century, almost. You built anything? Who've you loved? Got a wife? Children? Why not stay here?"

> You got no money,
> You got no home,
> Spinning Wheel all alone . . .

"Because I haven't done those things yet."

"You haven't shown many signs of ever doing them, either."

"So I haven't had much chance."

"And if you get one and you still don't do anything, how are you going to explain that?"

"I'll manage."

"And what if you can't handle it?"

> Did you find a directing sign
> On the straight and narrow highway . . . ?

But after a while we stopped talking, and I started being underwater. No more wondering about my back tangling in barbed wire or draping over concrete. Dark and quiet. I couldn't even feel the grenades going off anymore, it was so peaceful. Or see any reason to move. Or to check my body. Whatever was hanging out would turn the stomach of a corpse.

"You didn't escape, you know. You'll have your explosion. But not tonight."

Years later, when my daughter was born, time opened up a little, and I saw what he meant. And I saw when. I didn't want to see anything else.

But in the end I did check my body. To find out about myself. And because maybe that's where the answer was. I ran my hands over myself. I was all there. And properly arranged.

It must have been a TNT bomb.

It came time to swim for air, but I couldn't tell up. All those stories about drowning people struggling to the bottom.

"You had something you were planning? People who need you? Somebody to meet? Someone to love? Up and at 'em, Troop."

Someone is waiting just for you,
Spinning Wheel spinning true.

I thought maybe that was Linda. Or an unborn child. At least at first it was Frank Tubb.

The tightness in my chest was growing impatient when I bobbed to the surface. A good night for a life jacket.

Drop all your troubles on the riverside,
Catch a painted pony on the spinning wheel ride.

■ BOBBING ON THE BOW

THE WATCHES OF THE NIGHT

Waves smacking waves in brown turmoil. Movement without pattern. Slaps and splashes and hard-edged little ripples. I'd never known TNT bombs were so powerful.

My glasses were gone, and it was dark. Only the bow was left from my boat, jutting up like a shadowy grave marker. I scrambled on as best I could and attached myself to a stanchion. The big engines were finally drinking their fill.

I had been tied to pier number two when I was hit. Now I was on the other side of pier number three. I couldn't see how I had gotten there, past concrete and steel, barbed wire, and sandbags. I still can't.

Maybe I came skipping out like a flat stone, curling across the water. Maybe. But I don't believe it.

> Amazing grace, how sweet the sound
> That saved a wretch like me.
> I once was lost but now I'm found,
> Was blind but now I see.

However I got there, it was none of my doing.

> Through many dangers, toils and snares,
> I have already come.
> 'Twas grace that brought me safe thus far,
> And grace will lead me home.

If there was a reason for it, then maybe the reason will keep me safe next time. It was out of my hands. And if it was just luck, then what the hell? Maybe I'll be lucky again.

Either way, might as well do as I please.

■ LEAVING ON A CHOPPER

I hung from the bow, my eyes as dark as the shadows, marveling at being alive. Everything was so peaceful. The grenades had stopped falling. Even the water had settled down. Nothing but warm lapping.

Then a roar and a splash and a lurch and a boat was next to me. We bumped together in the waves it brought until Frank pulled me aboard and launched us toward the far shore. I rolled back like an unsecured cask and then crabbed off the front when we slammed into the bank. Frank got out with me.

"Jeez-us. You look awful. All that blood."

"Blood?"

I didn't feel any blood.

"It's all over you."

"It's the river."

"It's blood. Even this river ain't that thick. Check your hair."

Some stinging on top and my hand was sticky. Scalp wounds bleed a lot. But they'd just sew it up. My foot was what bothered me. Some bastard would probably try to set all those little bones. It was going to hurt like hell.

But Frank wasn't thinking about my foot. He was sightseeing.

"Jeeze, look at that bridge. Busted it like a tractor through a rail fence."

"Just a TNT bomb. Some fucking Arvin."

"MIGHTY GOD DAMN BIG TNT bomb. Look over there. LOOK."

I squinted after shapes in the darkness. Between Frank's pointing and the full moon I could make out the dark bridge against the sky and I could see the place where the sky dropped all the way to the water, where no bridge broke its fall. The tines of a naked pier jabbed where a tank filled with young American lives had rested.

The bridge had been a gift from the American people to the people of that tattered land. A dowry to be used in peace and freedom. When I left, it was wreckage. No use for travel and a hazard to navigation. The peace and freedom were just other people's dreams.

236 We stared for a while. Then Frank went to get the others. He left

me sitting with my back to a low wall of sandbags. He had the last
boat. The only way we had to get across the river.

Alone, in an unknown place, with a broken foot and propped against a wall. Crippled of vision. Muddy, bloody, and wet. But I knew something. Charlie had blown the bridge, and he was coming back. Human waves.

I kept telling the wolfhounds. But they wouldn't answer.

And then I had another thought.

Maybe they couldn't hear me.

Maybe I was as dead as George Kirby, my parts scattered along the Song Saigon. Maybe only Frank Tubb could see me. Or hear me. Poor Frank. He must have been standing too close. God knows where he'd gone. I was glad I hadn't gone there with him.

After that night, the thought kept coming back that I'd died in the explosion. I'd be out on the highway or alone in a motel, and I'd think maybe I wasn't there. Maybe my bones were rolling in the mud at the bottom of the Saigon River. Once, when I was on an airplane and an engine blew up, the thought came over me that I had nothing to worry about. That it was too late to kill me.

From then on, the idea followed me around like a cloud of gnats that maybe I was dead. But sitting there on the river bank that night I heard a thrumming. I looked, and behold, a whirlwind came out of the north. A chopper, its dark form and the blur of its blades round against the night sky.

> Ezekiel saw de wheel,
> Way up in the middle of de air,
> Ezekiel saw de wheel,
> Way in de middle of de air.

For a little while, medics darted among us. Then the chopper rose in a swirl of grit, cutting circles in the darkness.

> Ezekiel saw de wheel of time,
> Ev'ry spoke was of humankind,
> A wheel in a wheel,
> Way in de middle of de air.

It faded out over the river as another came in, turning the night.

O de big wheel run by faith,
An' de lit'l wheel run-a by de grace of God,
A wheel in a wheel,
Way in de middle of de air.

More medics choosing among us. More hoisting of stretchers and another chopper filled with living American flesh roaring away in a cloud of sand that would have blasted the paint from an APC.

When it quieted, I could see Frank. And Short and Sergeant Stamford. So it got them, too. Damn.

Wasn't much to say. And nobody tried to say it. But just as another chopper turned across the river, Frank yelled over the noise.

". . . stuck over here now. Tore up my boat on the God damn log boom. Ran it right over the mother fucker when I was going after you. Half full of water when I left here. Got back just as it went under . . . "

The new chopper cut him off. Grit started to fly again. Short and Sergeant Stamford covered my face. Frank cupped both hands over my ears and shouted, one word at a time.

"I'M . . . TICKLED . . . PINK . . . JUST . . . TICKLED . . . PINK . . . YOU . . . HAD . . . YOUR . . . FUCKING . . . LIFE . . . JACKET . . . ON."

I love you, too, Frank Tubb.

Then I was hustled on board. I looked, but I couldn't see them anymore. Not Frank. Nor Short. Nor Sergeant Stamford. I never saw any of them again.

But I'm sure they watched me leave.

Ezekiel saw de wheel of time,
Ev'ry spoke was of humankind,
A wheel in a wheel,
Way in de middle of de air.
O de big wheel run by faith,
An' de lit'l wheel run-a by de grace of God,
A wheel in a wheel,
Way in de middle of de air.

We flew over darkness. Then points of light. Then down onto asphalt and stripes beside a low building. The first in a series of dreary medical facilities the army had waiting for me.

The door barged open and I slid out, hopping barefooted across rough asphalt. Inside, a medic helped me onto a metal table with a lip to keep the blood off the floor. Like a steak platter.

Somebody who may have been a doctor worked my foot. Then ordered an x-ray.

"Any other injuries?"

"Only the head."

"The head?"

"Where all the blood's coming from."

He looked at his hands and thought about the red on them. Then he traced it to my scalp.

"I'll sew it up. Have to shave some hair off first, though."

He used a razor he'd been scraping paint with. And the same hand motions, peeling back the hair along with my dignity. Then he sewed the cut with an upholstery needle and was gone.

I waited on a vinyl chair in an empty room until a medic trotted in with my x-rays. He looked like he was bringing me a Christmas present.

"Whoo-whee. Going to Japan."

"What?"

"JAPAN. You done bought yourself a ticket out of the Nam."

"Two days I'll be back at the bridge."

"No way. You look here."

They did look bad. Bones snapped off like broken pencils. Shattered fragments lodged in the flesh.

"Ain't nobody got no use for no troop with no foot like that," and he grinned at me, "nohow."

"They're gonna make me a typist."

"You just look at them x-rays, Mr. Typist. Wish they was mine. Shee-it."

I knew he was right. But I didn't believe a word of it.

■ IN-COUNTRY HOSPITAL

Billowing up slowly from a brown sleep.

> Woke up, it was a Chelsea morning.
> And the first thing that I saw
> Was the sun through yellow curtains
> And a rainbow on my wall.

Of all the pleasures of the bed, waking up gradually is the sweetest.

Medics clanked things on trays. People talked softly, and I was reassured.

Trays of pills. Bright colors rattling in little cups. We drank them with orange juice.

> Red, green and gold to welcome you,
> Crimson crystal beads to beckon.
> Oh, won't you stay? We'll put on the day.
> There's a sun show every second.

Alive and in a clean bed.

> Woke up, it was a Chelsea morning
> And the first thing that I knew
> There was milk and toast and honey
> And a bowl of oranges, too.

And no C rations, thank you very much.

Standing full in the sun after living so long in the shadows. It was a good feeling. I wanted to hang onto it. I thought it was only a matter of will. Just hang on hard enough.

Slow and stretchy and nothing to do but television.

The other side of the world from D.C. In Washington it was election night, November 5, 1968. For us it was the morning of November 6. We watched last night's returns as they took place.

Two rows of narrow beds backed up to the walls in a narrow
240 building. Two rows of inmates risking permanent injury to their

necks stared all day at a TV bolted to the end of the ward. Wanting to know who would be president.

And nobody could tell. Not even Eric or Walter.

No answers. Just numbers. Precinct after precinct. The numbers wore into the afternoon, and the human eye couldn't see the difference.

I stared off to the left, holding my head in place with paralyzed muscles, straining at the fuzzy screen. Sometimes I'd roll onto my stomach and stare to the right, but you can't lie that way too long in a cranked-up hospital bed.

And into the evening. Some of the eastern states were 100 percent counted, and still nobody knew who was going to win.

Looking back, it seems strange we would have cared so much about that election. But we did. We were all brothers in a single hope. A single passionate prayer that Humphrey lose. That he be humiliated. We wanted it fervently. Ardently. We wanted it because he would sell his country to be president, the way he'd sold the war, three days before, when the polls showed it was expendable.

All of us wanted it. All but one. She was just twelve or thirteen, swelling into woman, and totally amputated. Nothing attached to her shoulders, nothing to her hips. Propped on pillows, she looked like somebody had left a guitar on the bed.

I never found out what had happened to her. She probably didn't know, either. She wouldn't have remembered. Just helping her mother in the kitchen or playing with her dad in the evening, racing about the house and giggling. And then surrounded by fierce strangers in a place where nobody spoke her language. Where somebody else had to rub her eyes and scratch her phantom itch itch itch itches. The only person in the room who couldn't just reach out and squeeze her growing breasts.

The election dragged into the night, and we went to sleep. We'd watched all day and we still didn't know who'd won.

I never planned to talk to anybody. I just wanted to think about how good the world was going to be. But I was interrupted.

"Pardner. Hey, pardner."

If I tilted my chin all the way to my chest and squinted down between my feet, I could just make out the pale oval of a face staring up at me. Somebody on the next stretcher down.

"Hey, pardner. We really headed for Japan?"

"That's what everybody says."

"Just worried maybe they've got an island someplace. You know."

"Not likely. I didn't diddle around with the local stuff. Didn't even punch on any doughnut dollies. I'm clean as a boiled rat."

"Don't reckon them sending you to no desert island, then. And I'm on the same plane as you. Heck. JAY-PAN BOUND. Don't mind telling you, pardner, I'd been worried about that one."

"So you got the Chinese clap?"

I was thinking about asking to be redeployed to the other side of the plane. The wing if it was vacant.

"Nah. Just frostbite."

"Frostbite? In the tropics?"

"Says frostbite right here on the tag."

A couple of medics wandered back to find out what the yelling was about. When they couldn't see anything, they wandered away.

"How'd it happen?"

"Shee-it. Everybody wants to know that. Sergeant. Captain. Even some damn colonel in the medical corps. And now you. Well, I'll tell you one damn thing. Them folks ain't never gonna find out. And you ain't neither."

"Maybe it's just some kind of injury."

"Frostbite. Says so right here on the tag."

"How'm I gonna read that, way down on the other end of your stretcher?"

"Well, you just look here at my toes, then. They ain't ordinarily black and shiny."

"I can't see black and shiny. My glasses are at the bottom of the God damn river."

"Well, when they unload us, pardner, you look then. And you read my tag, too. And you'll know this buckaroo caught himself the frostbite in this tropical fuckin' country."

They'd wake us up at 6:00 A.M. in the hospital. It was like a reveille. Lie in rows to be counted. Then back to sleep for as long as we wanted. On the morning of the third day, I woke back up and there was a tag on my bunk. Some bunks had them. Nobody would say what they meant. But we found out.

We were going somewhere. A knot of dark figures came with a fleet of rolling stretchers. One for each tag. We were hoisted out, strapped down, and wheeled off. As efficient as forklifts taking pallets from a warehouse. Only nobody tells the pallets where they're going.

Maybe a second-rate jungle hospital. I wasn't sick enough for a real one. Or dreary barracks and tedious work details.

Or maybe the island. The secret island where you go when you have the incurable VD. The place in the Trust Territories the government doesn't know about. Where they drop you and then tell your kin you're missing.

Maybe. But I didn't feel like I was a candidate for that place.

They hung us three deep inside a big green army bus. You can't shift yourself when you're strapped down like that and every bump hits you in exactly the same bruised and pulpy places. For hours.

People die in those buses. And on the planes later. Which is why the army gives them a few days to stabilize before shipping them out. Even so, there were no medical people on the bus, and when plasma tubes slid out of helpless arms, none of us knew what to do.

Bottles and bags and tubes swinging, puddles sliding over the floor, we bumped feet first into the unknown. I was on the middle rack, hanging over a window. But all I could see was the same rice paddies and palm trees that were outside every window in the country. No clue to what lay at the end of the road.

It was a big air force cargo plane stopped for some strangers headed to Japan.

> "Hi there, high line!
> Hello, highway!"
> Here comes a big old semi my way!

The cargo ramp snapped shut onto a belly full of Jonahs and the plane jerked forward and roared down the runway. In minutes we

were over the South China Sea. Out of the Nam for an unscheduled
R and R.

It was good to be gone.

> I've been a long time leaving here,
> But I'll be a long time gone.

Strapped to the bottom of an inside partition, I had the worst seat in the house. Cramped, dark, and no view. Like flying Eastern in the bathroom.

We rattled along in the gloom until the pilot throttled back for landing. Pardner began to worry again.

"You reckon they diagnosed you right? Maybe they think you've got the Chinese clap, too."

"Just says 'broken foot.'"

The ramp bumped down, and the cargo handlers began unloading us. Pardner was carried off ahead of me, like he'd promised. I got one frozen glimpse of toes sticking out of a tan Ace bandage. Shiny black toes. And on the tag, one word: "frostbite." Then they were by and down the ramp and Pardner was celebrating.

"YAHHHHHH HOOOOOO. IT'S JAPAN OUT HERE."

■ COMING HOME

■ DRIVE THROUGH YOKOHAMA

They left us stretched three deep in a green bus, in the care of two PFCs who must have lied about their ages to get into the army.

Sixteen and they drove like they had their first six-pack under the seat, bounding off curbs, sliding into intersections, and scattering Japanese. Sudden brakes. Clattering bottles and swaying tubes. Gut wounds and amputations and groans. No doctor and no nurse. Not even a medic. Nobody to take care of us except the two hot-rodders up front.

From the bottom stretcher I couldn't see much. Only the tops of things. Roof lines. Lampposts. Some vertical signs with Japanese characters and an occasional tree lunging to the rhythm of the bus. But no Japanese, no cars, no bicycles, even though people and traffic darted like goats around the bus. Life and commerce and activity just inches away.

We bumped and lurched through downtown Yokohama like we were on a dirt road, slamming through the red afternoon, praying the ride would end. Finally it did—or it seemed to. The bus stood swaying by the curb.

For a moment I thought the drivers were coming back to help. But they didn't. They walked away and left us on the side of the Japanese road.

Waiting with the sounds in the bus. A tube had torn loose from the arm just above me. It dripped slowly into the aisle, while blood braided its way down the arm to the wrist and into the palm and slipped from a finger, drop by drop.

In the end the drivers came back. It may have been forty-five minutes. Maybe it was an hour and a half. Then just back into the driver's seat and pop the clutch and never look back. They didn't notice the arm swinging over my stretcher. Or whose sutures had torn. Or who was still conscious.

We never learned where they'd gone.

Then another trip, crashing through the tops of Japan until, suddenly, our stretchers slapped forward, the bus hung on its brakes, and we rocked to a stop. The 106th General Hospital.

It was the only tour of Japan I would ever get.

■ THE 106TH GENERAL HOSPITAL

There was a riot around the hospital, but I couldn't see it from the bottom stretcher. Later, when I was cranked up in bed, my back to the window, I could hear it outside. A distant crowd chanting at a football game.

Sometimes I would turn around to it. Through the wire over the window, across the rooftops and to the edge of the compound. Two hundred. Two hundred and fifty meters. People hurling things. And slashing. And jabbing. Rushing in and out, white cloth around straight black hair. Dark symbols on bobbing signs. Angry. A place to be pulled apart.

I couldn't read the signs, and I couldn't make out the chants, but I could tell what they said.

YOU DIE, YANKEE PIGS

Later, I found out that mob had been out there for months. Formed up every morning at seven and raged till dark. All so organized it didn't seem like a riot at all. Just some kind of job action.

HOSPITAL PRIVILEGES FOR PODIATRISTS

■ SOCKS

I bought a radio from the hospital PX and lay earplugged into the American station. It filled up my thoughts, and nights it kept me off the river. Other nights I wandered around in the dark. Or sat by myself in the little room between the place where they kept us and the next ward. It was hardly more than a passage for orderlies and visitors, but once a distraught redhead, the wife of somebody stationed in Japan, backed in just before lights out and sat on one of the hard, high beds, stirring around in a basket.

"I really loved these socks. I really did."

"Socks?"

"But he didn't have any feet. What am I going to do? HE DIDN'T HAVE ANY FEET."

"You gave him socks?"

"I just wanted to do something for him. For all the brave men. So I made these socks. It gets cold here. I wanted them to know I loved them.

"They had such a good time when I brought them onto the ward, joking and throwing them at each other. When I got to him he was still asleep and I gave him a little shake. 'Hey, sleepy head. Want some socks?'

"'Sure,' he said. 'I'll take two of each. Wear them like mittens. Got any with thumbs in them?'

"Then he pulled back the covers and his legs just tapered down like baseball bats.

"HE DIDN'T HAVE ANY FEET. WHAT AM I GOING TO DO?"

■ SOLDIER WITHOUT LEGS

I t hurts SO much. OH, MOMMEEEEEEEE."
Part of him was in a private room down on One West. The rest was back at Cu Chi, scattered around the PX.

We heard him weeping on the phone. All the way home to the States.

"Mommy, I can't stand it."

Later we found out who he was.

"A regular by God troop. Set off a claymore in the PX. Stood it under a chair and sat down. Then just pulled the string.

"Guess he wanted to make an impression. Well, he sure impressed the next of kin. Had three of them here already.

"Only thing, when he pulled the string he didn't die.

"Must have been a clerk or something. Thought claymores exploded up, I guess. But it didn't. Cut straight through his legs instead. Showered them all over the PX. Missed the rest of him sitting there in the chair.

"Too bad he wasn't bending over to tie his boot at the time.

"How many casualties you got here from your bridge? Eleven? Fourteen? Shee-it. There was twenty-three of us in the PX. Some hit a lot damn worse then me.

"That's something, ain't it. The God damn PX at Cu Chi. Like being killed after you get home. And Charlie never touched it. No rockets, no mortars, no satchel charges, no nothing.

"Got him cuffed to a bed now. Guess they think he might try to run off.

"You come across that pasty-faced dog turd, throw me a favor. If your bladder's empty, spit on him for me."

■ JAPANESE TELEVISION

The wrestler turned over in an airplane spin and SLAMMED down to the mat. Japanese television on Saturday morning. It reminded me of home.

". . . had us on the Saigon River. Patrolling downstream at first. Then just sort of hanging around the bridge."

One of the wrestlers was bouncing on the ropes and waving his fist.

"Shee-it. Wouldn't catch me out on one of them boats. It's a wonder you didn't get a trip home, air freight. When I walk into an ambush I like to be able to find some cover."

Somebody we'd never seen before had the referee backed into a corner. The announcer seemed very excited about it.

"Nothing much ever happened."

They were loose in the studio, throwing wooden chairs at each other. When the show came to an end, they stopped and bowed. Thank God these people never found out about roller derby.

"Listen to the dude. River's infested with Charlies. They got rockets and heavy machine guns all along the banks, and he says nothing much ever happened."

Dark ships trailing evil music streamed toward the horizon. Saturday morning cartoons.

"Charlie didn't mess with us. We were bad."

Rows of tiny planes zoomed into the sky.

"Mr. Charlie ain't scared of nobody. What's somebody like that care about living?"

Fuel low, they searched over the foggy ocean.

"Well, he never bothered us any."

At last, a hole in the clouds. And dark ships below.

"Except at the end, I bet. Then he really let you have it, didn't he. Shee-it. He was just setting your ass up."

The planes spun down and SLAMMED into the ships.

"BASTARDS."

"What?"

"Those ships. They're us. Look at those kamikaze mother fuckers.

"Those bastards. THOSE YELLOW BASTARDS."

251

■ MAIL FROM HOME

The mail brought me a present. A good knife. A long blade to cut ropes out of propellers.

And something more. A Polaroid of Phu Cuong bridge the morning after I left. A freak coincidence shot taken by an old friend of my dad's. They hadn't corresponded in twenty-five years. The friend was still in the army. He'd seen the smashed bridge, taken a picture, and thought of my father. No particular reason. He hadn't even known I was in Vietnam.

My father just passed the picture on to me as a curiosity. He didn't know it was my bridge. Even so, it found its way to me as truly as if an AK47 had shot it through my heart.

■ SENT HOME

Two weeks in a Japanese government quarantine and then Japan. Gardens and pearl divers and shrines and bonsai nurseries and bullet trains and national parks waiting for the fifteenth day.

On the fourteenth day I was sent home. An air force sergeant wired a tag to my bed.

"CONUS. You're going Stateside."

"What?"

"Tet."

"I was in Basic then."

"Gonna be another one. Gonna need these beds. Would have sent you home sooner, but too many was dying. Got to wait fourteen days, now. To stabilize."

Bad luck. Or bad planning. Or maybe the Japanese just didn't want to see us.

■ LEAVING ON A JET PLANE

The cargo hold of a C-141. It was like riding in a boxcar. All bumps and no view.

And noises that seemed to mean something. Noises that slapped at us like pistol butts.

CLLPPPPP

A piece of sheet metal tore from the wing and

BLLPPP   BLLPPPPP   BLLLLPPPPPP   BLLLLLPPPPPP

Slapped back along the fuselage.

A strange place for combat soldiers who lived by listening—always listening—for danger.

GUGGGGGGGGGGGLLLLLLLLLLLL

Fluid sucked from a broken hydraulic line.

November 22, 1968. The fifth anniversary of the day Kennedy was murdered. We'd been strapped in our stretchers so long we were frozen in place. At 4:30 that morning they'd first rolled us down to the hospital lobby. To wait. Then we'd been bused to the airstrip and parked on the apron to wait again, like a load of turkey dinners set out to meet a passenger flight.

Our plane arrived at nine o'clock. Enormous, with a ramp gaping like the dark highway to Hell.

It took another hour to load up. We spent five and a half hours strapped in a flat place before takeoff.

And then we blew a tire.

BMMMPPPPPPPP   Bmpppflpp   flppp   flppppp

We could hear it flopping down the runway.

Another seventeen and one-half hours strapped flat in the air. No
254 sitting up. No rolling over. No shifting around. Just the same hard

canvas jarring the same tender places. We might as well have been in tiger cages.

Funny. Except for the stretchers, going home from Vietnam was all so easy. Getting there had been the hard part. The hours in the induction center. The running and shining and polishing in Basic. The night maneuvers and impossibly heavy bridge panels in AIT. The arctic winter and the Missouri summer.

But getting home was just reading *Lady Chatterley's Lover* on a warm night.

Rttl Rttl ttl   RTTL TTL RT

The number two engine began to slip loose from its mountings.

The passenger door had a porthole about the size of a salad plate. It was our only view out but I couldn't see through it at all from my stretcher. When I guessed we were next to the Kuriles, I unstrapped and hopped over for a look. Textured clouds dazzling in the morning sun. A wasteland of white. Nothing had changed since my flight out.

It wasn't much of a look, but it was all I got. A major spotted me. A major, no less for being in the reserves, caught me by the door. Maybe he thought I'd gotten tired of the flight and was about to step outside. More likely he was just responding to a medical emergency.

PATIENT OUT OF CONTROL
PATIENT OUT OF CONTROL

He turned the buckles under where I couldn't reach them again and left me stretched out with thoughts of reserve officers.

CRSHHHH   FLLNPPPPPPP

Amateurs driving a plane that was tearing itself to pieces.

Sometime that morning we got our day back. We crossed the dateline, and it became November 21. Kennedy was alive again five years ago.

■ WIFE OF THE SECRETARY OF DEFENSE

Andrews Air Force Base. Airport to presidents.

We were arranged in a bright room, heads displayed on starched pillows like jewels on little cushions. Those with unseemly wounds were somewhere out of sight.

We were resting from the flight when the door jolted open and a short woman in a red-and-white-striped dress—a stocky pipsqueak of a woman—bugled over us like a medieval herald.

"Mrs. Clark Clifford, wife of the secretary of defense."

And there she was. Larger and middle-aged in her own red and white dress.

The two surged through the ward, the little pipsqueak woman always one patient ahead, stopping and turning at each bed like mechanical bears in a shooting gallery. And to every patient the pipsqueak woman announced:

"That's Mrs. Clark Clifford. Her husband is the secretary of defense."

And then Mrs. Clark Clifford was by my bed, asking me about my bandage. I answered, saying nothing, and she was off. Down to the next patient.

Nothing, really, to say to each other. And yet, maybe there had been something. Maybe if I had just explained to her that I hadn't been expecting her. That I'd just gotten out of the back of an airplane that had been falling apart and didn't know what to say, maybe we could have worked something out. Gotten together later. But I didn't explain, and the moment passed. Like the girls I almost kissed in high school, Mrs. Clark Clifford, wife of the secretary of defense, became just another I might have touched.

■ FLIGHT TO FORT GORDON

The next day we flew home. The last time I'd been in a C-123 I had been on my way to Cu Chi, flying over the soft silvers and greens of a country at war. The Carolinas were beautiful, too, but they took some knowing, the prickly browns and burned-up greens of trees and pastures in a dying November.

The hand of man lay differently there, too. Farms and fields running true to old survey lines, all right angles, set out in quarter sections and eighth sections and a few acres squared off around the house. The brown corduroy of last year's planting and the blackened stubble of harvested crops in that beloved peaceful land.

Fort Gordon, Georgia. The end of the line. They didn't have any more hospitals to bump me to, so they just sent me home. Leave with my parents, a month at a time. Then back to the hospital for a few days. Long enough to arrange the next leave.

Atlanta. Such a short time after I had left there. It might as well have been Vietnam, it was all so strange to me. Girls in pastel, tattling about their friends and boys they never seemed to like very much. Cotton candy society. What Loi's father had wanted for her.

Sometimes I ran into people I knew. We would talk about what was important to them. What they were doing in school.

". . . I forget. But it sure beats the draft all to hell, if you know what I mean."

I did know what they meant.

"So where you been hiding out?"

"Nam. I've been to Vietnam."

"Okay, been to Nam. Shit, you didn't flunk out, did you? That'd get you there for sure."

"No . . . "

"And jeeze, what happened to your leg?"

"Foot, it was my foot. Busted it up pretty good."

"So what happened?"

"Explosion."

"Explosion?"

"Like I said. Vietnam . . . "

"Come on, man. What did you really do to your leg?"

"Night patrol out under the bridge. They must have used a hundred pounds of C4. I was right on top of the . . . "

"Give me a break. You dump off your bike somewhere?"

". . . knew Charlie was coming, but nobody was willing to do anything about it. Just let him move on in. Blew the fucking bridge with me standing there like a by God observer."

"That old Rambler. You piled up that old Rambler of yours. Lord, what a heap. How could you tell you'd been in a wreck?"

258 "Guys hundreds of meters away were hit. Sixteen casualties,

and I was in the middle of it, like a piece of God damn shrapnel. And all I got was a broken foot."

"Basketball? Soccer? Am I getting warm?"

"Sent me all the way back to the States. I couldn't believe it. Such a trivial fucking . . . "

"So you going to tell me or what?"

"All right. I was in a boating accident. Is that what you want to hear?"

"I busted my leg water-skiing once. Hurt like blazes."

"Foot. It was my foot."

"Foot? How you going to break your foot falling off skis?"

"You're not."

■ CHRISTMAS SPECIAL

Back at Fort Gordon, waiting for my next leave. But first:

THE BOB HOPE CHRISTMAS SPECIAL

". . . first stop was Ton Son Nuit, the big airport outside Saigon. So many GIs have come through Ton Son Nuit that . . . "

"GIs? Wofo he be calling us GIs for, nohow? Just what mofo war he be visiting?"

"Then it was up to Cam Ranh Bay, where our boys defend the vital lifeline of supplies from home. In fact, so many supplies have come through . . . "

"CAM RANH? I took mofo R and R in Cam Ranh. Ain't no war there. Just beaches and bitches. Wish I'd been defending me some of that mofo lifeline shit."

"Then we moved even farther north. Up to Da Nang. During TET, Da Nang was one of the hottest places in the country, just ask any Charlie who tangled with the First Marines there. . . . Many of those faces belong to men who beat Charlie back that day. In fact, they beat Charlie so far back . . . "

Bob wound back down through the country and finally arrived at a place I knew.

". . . of the Twenty-fifth Division. So much ordnance is fired at the airstrip here that the men call it 'rocket alley.'"

"ROCKET ALLEY? You ever hear tell of any Rocket Alley shit?"

A couple of the others had been with the Twenty-fifth, too.

"Not me, man. Tell me what the mother fucker's talking about. We always called it the airstrip."

"Beer cans. Maybe he's thinking about beer cans. Beer Can Alley."

"You was there!"

"Damn straight."

"Gimme five, bro."

"You dudes just shut up and watch that freckly bitch over to the left."

"Oh, shee-it. I remember her. Just look at that what she's going to do with her hand there."

It was hard to watch her hand. Bob Hope kept getting in the way.
And other people. And seas of faces. And when we could see it, it
was clapped tight to her side.

And then the troupe was off to Vung Tau and we never saw her
again. What she'd done in front of ten thousand drooling troops she
couldn't do on Georgia television.

That was how Bob Hope squeezed twelve shows into a single
Christmas hour. He left out the dirty parts. Just the opposite of the
news specials that left out everything about the country that was
whimsical or decent or hopeful and only showed the dirty parts.

■ EDGE

It was during Nixon's inaugural. I drifted off to sleep in the hospital, watching Marine Corps bands and motorcades. And I woke. To terror.

My eyes snapped open, trying to focus on a brown shape too close to see. A glazed doughnut. It scared hell out of me.

Vigilance. The legacy of the combat soldier. Quick as a mongoose, and you couldn't get within ten feet of me while I was asleep. It was my edge.

And that afternoon it was gone. Somebody had laid a doughnut on my pillow while I was asleep. Somebody had gotten in to me. It could have been an enemy soldier. But it was only a Red Cross volunteer who didn't want me to miss out on anything.

I never got it back. Sometimes I thought I had it, but all I had was an attitude. An ambition. And edges aren't the children of attitudes. They are born of circumstances, and the circumstances changed.

■ NEWS FROM THE WAR

The *Atlanta Constitution*, Tuesday, January 23, 1969. Wars and rumors of war. Occasional items I could recognize. Once, on a far inside page, something close to my heart.

"American and South Vietnamese casualties were reported heavy as 250 to 400 Communists overran the Twenty-fifth Division Base Camp at Cu Chi. Their immediate objective is thought to have been the helicopter pad located directly behind. . . . "

Raymond and the guy on the shelf.

"At this time it is not known how many of the big choppers were destroyed, but a spokesman for the Twenty-fifth stated that their loss would have no effect on the . . .

". . . also not known how many are still at large within the compound, and the base remains on full alert. . . .

". . . stigation has already begun into how so many enemy soldiers could have passed undetected through the wire."

I knew.

I knew how they got in. They formed up in a friendly village outside the gates, crept underground, and then streamed up through a well nobody could see.

And the thing I'm most sure about is that the sergeant who refused to look at the tunnel was not there when the enemy came. In the moment of danger someone else was standing with his back to the invasion.

■ WAR STORIES

When I was a kid, the funniest stories I ever heard were told by survivors of a Stalag. Real knee slappers. Three years and a jolly good time. Made me want to enlist as a POW.

Now it was my turn to tell stories.

Mrs. Brentnall came by one day. The army had told her where I was.

She was teaching her children gritty things. Things not in the standardized curriculum. She was teaching them about war, so she had them write to soldiers. A class project she'd been lucky with. The first soldier had been killed. And then I'd been wounded. Good lessons.

Now she wanted me to talk to them. Tell them what it was like. Stories.

And I couldn't do it. I couldn't tell those kids about Tony Paradise and Mudball the dog and what it felt like, watching a gunship at night, and not tell them the rest of it. That trick had been played on me.

And I wasn't ready to tell them about Hope Cook or Eraser Tits or the woman in the rice paddy. I didn't understand them myself then. So I did what I could. I told Mrs. Brentnall I'd write it all down when I'd gotten it figured out.

I've thought about it a lot since then. And I've written most of it down now. That's what all this is.

It took me a long time. Those kids are grown up now. They're older than I was when I came home. But I thought maybe if they could remember their class project when they were in the fifth grade, they would still like to know.

■ GIFTS

There was a mystery about her, something that had happened in Turkey. She wouldn't say what. We only knew about it at all because she came home from Europe two weeks early and without her motorcycle.

She had been Sam's girl for years, but she wouldn't tell him what had happened. She wouldn't tell anybody. Only me and then only when I got back from Vietnam. Something to look forward to. It was a sweet thought, and I thought sweetly on it.

And then I was back. We met in Blairsville. She and Sam and I. From there we walked on the Appalachian Trail toward Brasstown Bald to the cliffs overlooking Chattahoochee Springs. A tough day hike.

We looked out over laurels like small trees and rhododendrons as big as oaks to where the polished river curved around the rim of soft mountains.

It was wet up there. Mist rolled through the trees. Rocks dripped with small waters. Everything was green under mosses and little ferns. Somewhere a waterfall roared through the hills.

She sat between us, her knees pressed tight together, looking away. Then she turned to me, and all I had to do was ask. But I kept seeing that sweet American wife, pawing through her basket of socks, embarrassed by what she had given. And I couldn't do it any more than I could ask her to take off her shirt. I stood up, and we headed back down the trail.

■ FLIGHT TO FORT ORD

A LL ABOARD FOR FORT ORD, where I was stationed after I got out of the hospital. I flew there on April 12, 1969, the day the 33,641st American fell in Vietnam. The day the casualties exceeded those of Korea.

■ GARRISON DUTY

We must have been the first soldiers in history to come home to garrison duty.

It was like being in Basic again, and we didn't take well to it. Especially inspections.

Only our lockers stood at attention. Toothbrushes and soap made little blue and yellow puddles on the towels. Our socks and underwear were stacked in wrinkly heaps. We had grown suspicious of officers poking around behind us.

"What's he doing back there, Lou?"

"Don't know for sure. Might be looking at your underwear."

"Geez, what kind of man looks at another man's underwear? He isn't smelling it, is he?"

"Can't tell. He's leaning over mighty close, though."

"I've heard about guys like that. Don't like the idea of one walking around behind me. He could sneak up, and no telling what he might do."

"Just be sure not to bend over."

"Maybe we could get a butterfly tattooed on his dick. Sort of as a warning."

"Maybe he's already got a butterfly tattooed on his dick."

"I can't hear him anymore."

"He's down by Dave's locker now. Doing the same thing he did in yours. WATCH YOURSELF, Dave."

"I thought this kind of thing only happened in boardingschools. How'd that guy wind up here?"

"God told you you could die in Vietnam or you could come to Fort Ord. It'd cost you about the same. Wait until you find out what the cooks do in the back of the mess hall with the mashed potatoes."

■ PURPLE HEART

From how long it took my Purple Heart to catch up with me, you would have thought the whole Twenty-fifth Division had been overrun and not just the Chinook pad out by the wire. But one day it was mine. In a ceremony on a dusty stage in front of an empty theater. Seven men in a row and I was on the end. The other six had never gone past the gates at Fort Ord and had come to collect good conduct medals: to have red and white ribbons hung from their chests. The colonel who did the hanging said something to each that I couldn't hear, shook six hands, and was in front of me. He stood close and lingered. Then he leaned forward like he was going to kiss me. But he just pinned the medal on. Then he grabbed my hand and said, softly enough so nobody else could hear,

"Congratulations, son. I hope you win many more of these."

Sometimes I think that colonel just had his tape deck on automatic. He'd repeated the same phrase to six people with good conduct medals, and when he came to the seventh person in line, the one limping from a three-quarters-of-a-year-old wound, he just spilled out the same message.

Sometimes I think he knew what he was saying. He meant to say it, and he was the colonel. Who was going to tell him no? A flight of middle-aged whimsy. Or institutional arrogance.

"I tell you, Jack, those dumb shit enlisted men never listen to a thing you say. Why, just this . . . "

When he was done, he did an about-face, and that was it. The ceremony was over, and the seven of us were left staring at one another.

Back at the barracks I ran into Ike Handy. He'd never gotten a Purple Heart.

"Never even got scratched. And I saw some real shit over there, too. Patrolling all the time. Be out for a month, Charlie all around. Then in camp for a few days and back out for another three or four weeks. Ambushed. Hit at night. Zeroed in by mortars. Cut off and spent two days in a ditch until an APC came by. Must have been a firefight a week."

"Jesus. You pulled a whole year of that?"

"Ten months. I couldn't stand it anymore. Bought my way out."

"What?"

"Re-upped with choice of duty station. This is my choice."

"What did it cost you?"

"Three years, four months. They make you sign up for four years, and the four years don't start running until you re-up.

"Something, huh? They send you where you're bound to get killed, and they make you buy your way out by taking a job away from some other poor fucker who'll go to Vietnam in your place. With a four-year re-up you'll send three guys to Nam. Bloody good exchange for the army."

"Was it worth it?"

"Maybe. Three weeks after I left, my squad walked into an ambush. Bang. Every one of them blown away. Gone. I was the only one left."

"Jesus."

"I was down for R and R that week. But lot of guys get bumped, so who knows? One thing I do know. I'm glad I'm here now."

Houston, Tranquility Base here. The *Eagle* has landed."

We'd stayed up all night to watch it. Walter Cronkite had stayed up all night, too, to tell us about it. And Arthur C. Clarke had stayed up all night as well. To tell *Walter* about it.

When you came right down to it, Walter Cronkite didn't know a moon shot from Shinola, so CBS hired Arthur C. Clarke as a sort of on-the-air consultant to help him out. And Arthur did admirably . . . for the first eighteen hours or so. But it was a long flight to the moon, and his body was still on Sri Lankan time. He hadn't cut his teeth on all-night election coverages like the news heads all around him.

Under the circumstances, Arthur C. Clarke did what he had to do. He went to sleep, propped up behind the big desk next to Walter. The picture narrowed down so that only Walter was showing. All we had of Arthur were occasional contented snuffles.

Until Walter had a question.

". . . will tell us why Mike Collins has to remain in orbit aboard Columbia instead of descending to the lunar surface with the other two astronauts."

Then Walter's hand would snake out the left side of the screen and Arthur would make a bubbling noise and you could hear him straighten himself up. Then a little whisper, the screen would open up, and there would be Arthur C. Clarke, gathering momentum.

When Arthur was done, Walter would step in with a line of air-filling monologue and Arthur would glaze over as the picture narrowed back down.

And that's the way it was, filling time until Neil Armstrong could wade in with a heavy-booted foot, stepping off the ladder:

"That's one small step for man. One giant leap for mankind."

That's what he really said, foot to the moon on July 20, 1969. "One small step for man." Not "a man" or "one man." Not even "this man." Just "man." With maybe a billion people watching, Neil A. Armstrong, an American astronaut and the first human being to set foot on the moon, blew his lines.

270   They'd wanted him to get them right. Nobody wanted him step-

ping out on the moon and casting about in his subconscious for something to say.

"Well, I'll be dipped in shit. That politically bound-up space agency and all those candy-assed engineers got me here after all. And Yuri and John and Alan and all you other peckerwoods back on Earth, whose name are the kids going to be memorizing in school now?"

So they gave him a secret phrase to memorize. A vacuous little sentiment adjusted away to nothing so as not to offend anybody. Just enough to trip over when the time came.

And in tripping over it, what he said was better.

"I can't fucking believe I'm here. All those years of tight-assed discipline, and I'm still so knocked over I've forgotten what I was supposed to say."

In time, Edwin Aldrin came down the ladder and joined him, and two grown men hopped around the lunar surface like happy gerbils, pretending to be there for some scientific reason.

Then the screen split and the *Eagle* and men shrank to the right. On the left was Nixon, exulting in the culmination of Kennedy's space program.

After a while, even he switched off, and the astronauts, their air packs running low, climbed back into the *Eagle*. We were cut back to CBS Central and Walter and the big desk.

No more partial shots. The desk filled the screen. Walter's side. Arthur's side. Walter. A picture of the moon. And nothing more. No Arthur and no explanation.

We never found out what happened. Had Arthur's contract just run through the first moon walk? Had he been dumped in mid-program, and were CBS lawyers at that very moment preparing a complaint? Maybe he'd just slid under the desk and nobody could figure out how to get him out without creating a disturbance. Whatever, it was one of those situations that WE DON'T TALK ABOUT, and Walter never mentioned him again.

■ RUBBER LEG

He picked up the rubber leg during Tet. Three AK47 rounds in his thigh. Surgery before he left III Corps, straps and buckles in Japan. He thrust his hip and swung his way into a discharge at Fort Lewis.

I ran into him sitting in a bar in Monterey, perched on a stool in front of the television, talking loud to a couple of civilians.

". . . always been like that. I tell you, four or five brews and I go numb. You can drive a ten-penny nail right through it and I'd never feel a thing. . . .

"Sure, I'd do it, only I haven't had the beers yet.

". . . well, I'd like to, but I don't have the bread. Now, if you gentlemen could . . .

"Deal. The bartender here will set up five beers. . . .

"I know I SAID four or five, but I don't want any accidents. Like I said, the bartender will set up five beers and hold my watch here. When I'm done, I'll run that long steel needle he's got there right through my leg.

"If the needle doesn't come out the other side, you get to hock the watch. Either way I keep the beer."

He gulped the first beers and then grew thoughtful. Time wore slowly on, marked only by the coming of the eleven o'clock news.

". . . death was announced today. . . . no one outside Hanoi, and possibly no one even there, knows for sure who will succeed Ho Chi Minh. . . . The effect of today's events on the outcome of the war is difficult to gauge at this . . . "

"Well, shit."

He spat into an empty glass.

"I thought he'd never die."

The others didn't care about that, though.

"So drink, the son of a bitch, and let's get on with it."

He raised his glass and drained it right in front of the screen, blocking pictures of muddy, trampled land so littered with garbage it looked like a sanitary landfill.

". . . two weeks later are still cleaning the farm outside Bethel, New York where the festival was held. Participants . . . "

"I believe my leg is sufficiently numb, gentlemen. MAY I HAVE THE NEEDLE, PLEASE."

The bartender brought it out in a long blue box, like a dueling pistol. He took it and raised it high with both hands, then with a yell he flashed it down and sank it about halfway into his leg. Stuck in bone, I guessed.

"The bet is, gentlemen, that the needle must come out the other side. Bartender. Do you have a toolbox on the premises?"

The bartender handed him a big steel hammer and he drove that needle until the head was buried in his pants leg.

". . . Angeles County Coroner, Thomas Noguchi, today revealed further details of the ritual mutilation of Miss Tate and her four com . . ."

It gave me the willies, but all of us kept staring. Until somebody figured out the trick.

"It's a fake, you rotten son of a bitch. That needle's too long to fit in your leg. You got a trick needle like magicians use. I'm going to stuff that hammer down your fucking throat."

"The bartender gave me the needle, for Christ's sake."

With that, the man with the needle tried to slide off the stool but was stuck.

Then the man who knew it was a trick reached up under the stool.

"Geez."

And he found the needle sticking out below two inches of solid fir seat, flickering red in the light of the beer sign.

"I'll have to have the pliers."

"Easier to cut it off with a hacksaw first."

It wasn't until later, when he worked himself loose and then pitched his hip toward the door, that I saw him walk. And I knew what he'd done. Nobody else noticed. Or even wondered where the blood went.

I asked him about it out in the parking lot.

"It was the embassy. Charlie overran the bottom two floors, we came in on the roof. By God helicopter assault teams on our own damn embassy.

"I was one of the first in. Ran point down the stairs. Kicked open a door. Room full of Charlies and some embassy people. I shot up three magazines getting those people out of there.

"Kicked open the next door and ran into an AK47 burst. Got a silver star out of it.

"You know what, though? What I kept thinking on those stinking stairs all choked up with smoke? I kept thinking Ho Chi Minh was an old son of a bitch and he was going to live longer than me.

"I got out of it, though. Came home, got a new leg, learned to walk again, and that ain't all I've learned. I can dance, too.

"This war ever ends, I'm going to go to Hanoi and find Uncle Ho's grave. And I'm going to dance and dance."

■ DISCHARGE

A nd one day it was over. The first sergeant shook my hand and it was like he had waved a wand. I turned from a toad into a civilian. Brass buttons sparkled on the floor when I ripped off my jacket.

Having no plan, I drifted north and east. Over the mountains into the desert.

Nevada. Where you could stand in the middle of wide valleys and look over sixty or seventy rolling miles of landscape with no fences to break the patchwork of dark pines dappling into the distance. Thunderstorms came crashing through there with an unbelievable drama, night black clouds surging through the low mountains, threads of sky blue as flame and the land a shining iridescent ocher that glowed from within like yellow stained glass.

I drifted east through days of rolling scrub and low mountains, not thinking where I was going until I crested one more ridge and looked down and out on a gleaming flatness that might well not have been on this earth.

Utah. A land of no life and no water. If it had ever rained there, the rain had turned to poison when it touched the bitter ground.

Emptiness held its attractions for me just then. I could walk off into that shining white land and say whatever I wanted. And say it loud, with no sergeant to hear.

I set out across the brittle salt crust toward a bluish white hill I thought was nearby.

I wanted to walk right up to it and spend the day there and come back that evening. But I couldn't do it.

In the clear air, the hill never got any closer. I got the creeps. After a while it was hard to make out where I'd come from. I worried I wouldn't be able to find my way back. It was a silly worry. My tracks were easy to see against all the white.

When I had gone as far as I dared, I stopped and looked around for listeners. There weren't any, and I laid back and yelled. I howled out all the things I hadn't been able to yell during the last two years.

I'd imagined a giant roar of outrage, but my voice just sounded thin against all that openness.

When I was done I walked back. I was a civilian, then, and filled with civilian concerns.

Sha da da da, Sha da da da da
Sha da da da, Sha da da da da
Sha da da da, Sha da da da da
Sha da da da, Sha da da da da
Yip yip yip yip yip yip yip yip,
Mum mum mum mum mum mum,
Get a job.

■ EPILOGUE

The news out of Southeast Asia never went away. It was Nixon's war, now, but Nixon didn't fight it any differently from Johnson. It was a proxy war fought by machines. It was Maxwell Taylor's policy: bombs from forty thousand feet. Our machines against their people, while we stayed home and thought of peaceful things.

But you can't win wars that way. Fighting has to be personal. The most we ever did, the closest we ever came, was partially destroying the house of the North Vietnamese negotiator in Paris. Too bad he wasn't home.

> Bang! Bang! Maxwell's silver hammer
> Came down upon his head.
> Clang! Clang! Maxwell's silver hammer
> Made sure that he was dead.

We couldn't keep it up. In the end we just quit. And the grinning barbarians overran Saigon. And all those people, all those millions of South Vietnamese, just dropped out of our minds.

Many of them hated us. Most probably just wished everybody with guns would go away. But an awful lot of them had fought alongside us. Those were the ones we left behind. Faces frantic to get out. Clinging to the skids of our choppers and pushed from the doors of our planes to vanish under the weight of the new order.

But as I think back on that time, a strange thing happens. My memory splits as through a crystal. All the big events—the bombings, the negotiations, the sad end of the war—all fade back into that dusty place where history seems inevitable.

But the personal things, the people, don't fade. They are as fresh in my mind as if we'd had breakfast together this morning.

I think about Loi, who wanted to be an American. And I think about Ha. What place has their new country made for them?

Sometimes, I wonder about the friends I left at the bridge. Tony and Frank and Sergeant Stamford. What became of them in the days after I came home?

Sometimes, in the middle of the night, I wonder whether I'm still   279 alive at all. Or whether I was scattered in the darkness back under the bridge. Maybe everything after the bridge is a dream and my broken bones are rolling in the yellow water, washing forever back and forth in the tide.

As the years passed, I found myself thinking about the war more. And sometimes, something would happen or I would meet somebody who brought it all back.

■ LOSER

I couldn't see him well. He was standing in the shadows in an alley.

"Got a quarter for a Vietnam veteran?"

"Come on, we're all veterans."

"No man, I really am."

"Who're you with?"

"Seventh. Around Saigon. Wasn't such a bad place. People in the field called in. We'd send the planes and the shells out.

"And then I was in the field for about six months. Grunt. On the floor. Walking around on the bottom. Worst thing I saw was Sammy step on a mine. We'd been buddies since I was twelve. Then one day he shot up in the air in little pieces. Wasn't any farther away than that sign there.

"That's what I remember most, I guess.

"Took a test then. After that I got to sit in camp and type.

"Came home, man. My bro got all my benefits."

"Your brother?"

"Yeah, man. My bro. I been drinking some.

"Had some trouble when I was growing up. Gangs. You know. The Bronx. That judge was going to put me away for three, four years. I was supposed to go back to get sentenced. Went to the army instead. But I was too young. So I took my brother's birth certificate into the recruiting station. Got his age. Got his name, too. For three years. When I got out he told me, 'Bennie, you been a good brother to me. Kept me from getting drafted. Now I'm taking my name back.' And he did.

"He spent the war in a packing house. Our uncle covered for him. I'd worked there before I went in. And my last day they had a little party. A few beers. A couple of J's. Then I was off. Goodbye, Bennie.

"You know, Nam was bad. But scaredest I ever was was on the streets back in New York.

"I got home to the Bronx and I was afraid the pigs'd be waiting for me. I hit the dirt running. First trip out to New York, I got together with my wife. Divorced her. Kept moving. I was in Iowa or some damn place when I got busted for speeding. Took me in. I   281 figured they had me, but the judge let me off on my O.R. Charges against me had expired. Can you believe that shit? Statute of limitations.

"That stopped me. I went to cash in on some of my veteran's benefits but they told me I hadn't never been in the army. They were for my brother, man.

"He's livin down in Encino, now. Got a wife, six kids, and a VA mortgage. And a college education he got on the GI bill. He got flying lessons, too, and runs a crop duster on weekends.

"Oh, man. My bro."

When I got the chance, I checked a list of units we'd had in Vietnam. There wasn't any Seventh Division. Not army. Not marine. Not anybody.

■ DOUGHNUT DOLLY

D on't fall in love with a soldier,' that's what they told us. 'You're here to do a job. Not to go home with some GI.'

"But what did I know about soldiers? I just wanted to help people. I'd been an activist in college and wasn't about to join the nursing corps. Make guys better so they could get shot up again. But being a doughnut dolly, what could that do for the war effort?

"I almost didn't make it, though, the Red Cross was keeping such a low profile about recruiting for Nam. They sent an interviewer to our campus, all right. But nobody saw her. All those big signs. 'GENERAL MOTORS.' 'ESSO.' 'IBM.' 'CITIES SERVICE.' But nothing for doughnut dollies. But my roommate found her somehow and told me. We were the only two she interviewed. I told her about the protests and what I thought of the war. Told her twice and wrote it on the form. But she didn't seem to care. Hired us both. They must have been having trouble with their quotas.

"We were based at Pleiku, but five days a week they flew us somewhere else. C-130 over to the coast. C-123 down to Saigon. Got as far north as Da Nang. One day a week we worked at Pleiku, and one day a week we got off. We'd see all those guys stuck in one place, fighting the war. They never knew what was going on. We just kept touring around. By the time I came home, I felt like I'd seen everything.

"Everywhere we went, we handed out little Red Cross sacks of stuff. Razors. Shaving cream. Things they could have gotten at the PX. Around Christmas we passed out ditty bags. Full of stuff the ladies back home made to help the war. Knitted socks. Gloves. Once I even saw a little pouch to hold a prayer book. Junk. Guys would open those bags and mostly look puzzled. Too polite to throw them away in front of us, though.

"They made us go to those little ceremonies where the colonel turned the battalion over to his replacement. There were a lot of those, and there were always a few words about what a great outfit it was and how they had killed almost five thousand VC in a sweep just last September and how they lined the bodies up and the colonel had personally counted them. After enough of those I resigned.   283

"That's another advantage the women had.

"I never fell in love over there. I played it straight. I thought I could do some good that way.

"The two women I shipped home with were following their fiancés. I think they let the men down. Not me, though. I did some good. If nothing else, the guys could look at me and remember there was something else."

It was funny, what she thought about herself. Not at all what we had thought about doughnut dollies.

■ THANKSGIVING

Thanksgiving: Our special American holiday when we thank
God for our prosperity and celebrate our freedom in our
own land.

I sat down next to someone I hadn't met. A Chinaman. A Red
Chinese come from the mainland to study American engineering
and American ways. We turned out to have something in common.
We were both veterans.

Vietnam veterans.

"You *fought* in Vietnam?"

"Yes. In 1968 and 1969."

"Were there many . . . ?"

"One hundred, two hundred thousand. Not so many for us."

I knew about the Chinese already, of course. From a warm eve-
ning on a bunker a long time ago with a black man who had counted
their bodies up near the Cambodian border. But still, 100,000 or
200,000 troops from Mainland China on the ground. A major land
war in Asia against the Chinese and our government never told us.

■ COMPETITION

When the war had receded far enough and we could see ourselves more clearly, we built a memorial to the people we had been and for those we had known. So they wouldn't die with our memories. We built it ourselves. No government funds.

We tried to do it right. To build a memorial for the people, not for some architectural elite. A national design competition open to all Americans. The ideas rolled in—over sixteen hundred entries. It became the largest design competition in history.

I was an architect by that time, and so I know. The contest was administered by the American Institute of Architects. The AIA chose nine judges, all of them accomplished architects. Most were fellows of the Institute. A blue ribbon panel that picked, for the winning design, a black wall in a hole.

A black wall designed by an architecture student at Yale. A girl who had previously submitted it for her course in funerary architecture and gotten a C on it.

The committee liked the design. They said it was minimalist. The veterans hated it and tried to organize to stop it. To change it. To make something different happen. But they were powerless against the mass certainty of the AIA.

The day the contract for the memorial was actually let, New York Avenue, outside the national offices of the AIA, was filled with veterans. Five thousand men, some actually weeping in the street, begging the committee to choose something else.

By then most members of the committee, locked away in the AIA tower, realized they had made the wrong choice. But a principle was at stake: the integrity of the AIA competition process. So they stuck with their decision. Architecture for architects. The client be damned. In this case, two million clients.

A black wall in a hole. A blatantly political statement dreamed up by a girl in a flat homage-to-Frank-Lloyd-Wright hat. A girl too young to have been paying attention when the war was going down.

■ AT THE WALL

When I had wondered enough about the people I had left in the war, I went to Washington to visit the memorial. To find the names written out there.

The wall was even drearier than advertised. A dismal cut in a low hill faced with black rock, concealed from three directions and obscured from the fourth. Big patches scrubbed from the frayed grass. The whole place was tied together by boardwalks. It looked like a construction site rather than a monument to two million soldiers in a cause we once thought important.

Black, subterranean, and hidden, it was a monument to only one aspect of the war: death. Where was the exuberance and moxie of the people I remembered? And where was their noise? It was all much too quiet for the people I had known.

The names were inscribed in the order in which their owners had died. A long black thread running through the war.

All those names but nothing about the people. They might as well have been serial numbers.

But still, the names kept their power. Separately, they were almost voiceless. Together they were eloquent.

There weren't any official guards at the memorial. Just veterans from around the country who camped out there to keep an eye on things. Dressed in showy camouflage fatigues, spit-shined boots, billed caps, and bushy black beards, they didn't look as we had during the war, all bleached and dusty. They looked like Castro.

It took me some time to understand. Those never-never outfits were VFW and American Legion. Men who had scorned their service ribbons when they had been awarded now wore them on their fatigue jackets, where they did not belong, in the pride of what they had once been.

And they saluted each other. Salutes that enlisted men would never have given each other in the service. Salutes that they had been proud not to have given anyone in Vietnam. All those men, every one of them, had relinquished this token of their passage through fire. They were willing to look to all the world like soldiers who had never left the States. And they did it to salute each other, as a sign of their respect. In the army, they had saluted the uni-   287

form, not the man. But at the monument, they saluted the man—
always the man.

There were guides at the wall, and they had alphabetical lists of
those who had died. Indexes to the names on the wall. A guide
handed me one, thick as a phone book. Name, rank, branch of
service, date of birth, home town, date of death. MIAs had a star
before their names, which meant only that they hadn't been dead
when they were last seen. They are almost certainly dead now.

The book lacked the presence of the wall but was more moving
in its way. You could glimpse a little of the person in it. If you saw he
was from Lakeland, Florida, or Pacific Grove, California, or from
West Bend, Wisconsin, you knew a little of what he had given up
when he did not come home.

And the guard never bothered you. He didn't ask for his book
back, and he didn't ask helpful questions. He just let you alone.

Jake Gyer.

Frank Tubbs.

Tony Paradise.

And Sergeant Halys.

And Sergeant Stamford.

And Calvin Rose.

And Phoz.

And Raymond.

And Perce.

And Nikiyama.

And the guy on the shelf.

And the guy from South Carolina.

I looked them all up but one. And of those I looked up, none was
listed. Nobody that had been with me was there. The only one I
found had been somewhere else. It was over, and I could stop
thinking about them.

All but the one.

I handed the book back to the guide.

"You looking for someone you couldn't find?"

"Yeah."

"That's good news."

"Almost. I did find one. But I was already pretty sure about
him."

"So now you know?"

"No, not yet."

☆MacDevitt, Samuel H., Capt., USAF, 20 Jul 1943, Charlotte, NC, 3 Oct 1968.

The guide left to offer his book to somebody else. But there was still one more name. One name I hadn't looked up. One name I was afraid to find.

"Afraid?"

"I'm not sure I want the answer."

"You've already got the answer. You wanted maybe a notice in the *Congressional Record?*"

"I'm alive?"

"Check the book, then forget this shit. It was washed off in the Saigon River. Leave it. You got things to do. You made some promises, you know."

The guard was back, holding out the book of the dead.

I leafed through it to the one name I had avoided before. I found the page and I found the line. The name wasn't there.

I closed the book and tried again. My name still wasn't there. THEY HAD MISSED ME. The sons of bitches had missed me.

> I'm gonna lay down my sword and shield
> DOWN BY THE RIVER SIDE,
> DOWN BY THE RIVER SIDE,
> DOWN BY THE RIVER SIDE.
> I'm gonna lay down my sword and shield
> DOWN BY THE RIVER SIDE.

"So much noise and expense. Why did we do it?"

"For you."

"For me?"

"So you wouldn't have to spend your whole life selling insurance. Sorry?"

"Hell, no."

> I ain't gonna study war no more.
> I ain't gonna study war no more
> DOWN BY THE RIVER SIDE,
> DOWN BY THE RIVER SIDE,
> DOWN BY THE RIVER SIDE,
> DOWN BY THE RIVER SIDE,
> DOWN BY THE RIVER SIDE.

■ CONCLUSION

S o, that's it, Mrs. Brentnall, it's all here. What I couldn't tell your class. I thought you'd want to read it. You're welcome to tell them as much of it as you like if you can figure out how to say part of it without lying about the rest.